An Even Better
Marriage

An Even Better
Marriage

START TODAY BE HAPPIER FOREVER

STEPHEN ARTERBURN

WORTHY®
Inspired

Library of Congress Control Number: 2015943303

To my wife:
You are giving me the best years of my life.
As my mother said before we married,
"Everyone should be married to someone like you."
Well, I am, and I'm so grateful.

Contents

—⊙—

1

— ⊙⊙ —

Embrace, Enhance, and Enjoy Friendship and Fun

To watch a short video on this subject, go to
7MinuteMarriageSolution.com/8

My wife and I love to dance! We are not the greatest dancers, but we dance. If we are in a shopping mall and the music is perfect for a swing and a twirl, then we take a break and dance. We have been known to dance our way to the top in a tight elevator while people sigh and laugh and say they wish they had someone to dance with. If the music that catches our ear is slow, we will dance slow. But we love faster tunes where we can twirl and spin under each other's arms. I fold her into me and then I spin her out. I lead, she follows, and for a few short moments the tough realities we face go away. We are each other's, and it is evident we enjoy being a couple.

When our kids are with us, I think they get a little embarrassed at our dancing. But I also think they secretly enjoy seeing the smiles on our faces and on those who stumble upon our romance. Now that our boys are teenagers, they are even getting into the act. We were at an open-air concert the other night and James, our thirteen-year-old, stood up and started dancing with his mom. It is contagious. And it is fun.

Fun in marriage is similar in many ways to romance. It keeps a marriage from going stale. It keeps couples connected in a positive and relational way. Fun is also similar to romance in that it is not something you merely tack on to your relationship as an extra; it is integral to the health of your marriage. Fun is more than just the icing on the cake; it is a vital ingredient in the cake itself. You need fun and humor in your marriage.

A little humor and fun may be
your best path to restoring or renewing
or revitalizing a relationship.

Now, I know that if you are in a stale or bitter state of marriage, the last thing you want to focus on is fun. I understand. It is not going to happen instantly or easily. But just think back to the early days of your relationship. What did you do then that was really fun for both of you? Was it something you have not done in years, like riding go-carts? Was it an event such as a live concert? Was it taking a walk in a favorite park? You must have done a number of things that created fun for the two of you.

Imagine what chill might be thawed if you engaged your mate in that fun thing from the past. Think of the message that would send. It would say that you remember and the memory matters to you. It would say that you are willing to try something risky or to look foolish if it might add a new dimension to the relationship or even shake it up a bit. Just the attempt at putting some fun back in your relationship could cause your mate to see you and your marriage in a new light. A little humor and fun may be your best path to restoring or renewing or revitalizing a relationship. It could do wonders for the romance of your marriage.

GOD WANTS COUPLES TO HAVE FUN

The most important similarity between fun and romance is that both are God-created. And as the following passages show, God deems fun and good humor to be vital ingredients to a full and healthy life.

- "A merry heart makes a cheerful countenance, but by sorrow of the heart the spirit is broken" (Proverbs 15:13 NKJV).
- "All the days of the afflicted are evil, but he who is of a merry heart has a continual feast" (Proverbs 15:15 NKJV).

- "A merry heart does good, like medicine, but a broken spirit dries the bones" (Proverbs 17:22 NKJV).

You think those old crusty Bible characters didn't have a little fun? You think they were all a bunch of uptight Torah thumpers? I am intrigued by an Old Testament passage as it reads in the King James Version: "And it came to pass . . . that Abimelech king of the Philistines looked out at a window, and saw, and, behold, Isaac was *sporting* with Rebekah his wife" (Genesis 26:8; emphasis added). Modern translations flatten out the meaning of the passage by substituting the words "caressing" or "holding" or "embracing" for the King James Version's "sporting." I presume that Isaac and Rebekah were not playing tennis, but somehow those softer and less vivid words in the new translations seem a far cry from that intriguing word, "sporting."

I was a bit mystified by the translators' use of *sporting* until I learned that in the Hebrew, the original word has the same root as Isaac's name, which means "laughter." Therefore, whatever else the word conveys, it must include laughter. In the context of that particular verse, the connotation is obviously sexual, but it goes further and characterizes the mood of the couple: Isaac and Rebekah were playful, laughing, and having a good time with each other.

If it has been a while since you and your spouse have sported with each other, then perhaps it is time to take a lesson from these playful patriarchs. Think back: Didn't many of the things you once did together lead to "sporting"? Did you ever compete in a game with each other and then fall into each other's arms afterward? Did you play pool or Ping-Pong and end up hugging and holding through a good laugh? Did you ride bikes or climb mountains and then find yourself falling exhausted in each other's arms? Whatever it was, give it another chance. Sure, you might look foolish and embarrass yourself a little. But if it gets the two of you out of your self-obsession and into the fun and laughter mode, who cares?

BEING A FRIEND WITH YOUR MATE

The idea that couples should have fun, laughter, and a good time with each other brings up an important facet of marriage—friendship between husband and wife. Surely you have heard this before, but let's review what friendship means. Friendship is one of four kinds of love that humans experience. Its biblical name is "brotherly love" (*philia* in the Greek). The other three loves are affection (the Greek *storge*), sexual love (*eros*), and sacrificial love (*agape*).

Affection is the warmth and tenderness we feel toward another being. The object of affection can be a family member, a friend, or a pet. Sexual love (*eros*) is to be directed only toward one's wedded mate. Sacrificial love (*agape*) is that deep love that sees the other as more important than the self and is willing to make great sacrifices, including one's life, for the other.

5

This love can be directed toward one's mate, family members, friends, or even toward animals. We learn much about the high value of marriage when we realize that it is the only relationship on earth that embodies all four of these loves.

Now let's hone in on the meaning of friendship, which has much to do with our focus in this chapter. When friendship is present in marriage, it differs from sexual love in that instead of the mates focusing on each other, both focus on a common interest. Lovers look at and are absorbed by each other. Friends look together at some interest other than themselves. Competent sexual lovers say to each other, "What can I give to you to increase your joy and pleasure?" (nothing wrong with that, but great marriages are great outside the bedroom. *More on this later*) Friends say to each other, "Let's direct our focus toward that object or activity we both enjoy. Let's have fun together."

That object or activity may be a game such as chess or tennis; it can be reading together or walking on the beach; it can be a project, such as planting a flower bed, painting a room, or designing a house; it can be a hobby such as restoring furniture or collecting first editions; or it can be something fun, like dancing, attending concerts, or camping. The point is that lovers focus on each other; friends focus on common things they like and enjoy. Both relationships are part of a vibrant and satisfying marriage. Too often a person focuses on how to be a better lover or how the other person could be a better lover when the answer starts with being a better friend first.

One reason romance tends to fade is that early in marriage we try to hold on to the intensity of romance without attending to the components that nourish romance. It's like picking flowers: When you cut flowers from their life-giving stalk and gather them into a spectacular bouquet, you achieve a momentary glory. But the flowers soon wither because they are cut off from their source of life. Romance grasped for itself is spectacular while it lasts, but it dies quickly if cut off from the sources that feed it. And one of those sources is friendship. To focus solely on each other to the exclusion of all else eventually wears thin. You must focus together on other sources of joy to keep the romance nourished. No one can long maintain a high level of emotional intensity. Variety in focus enhances the marriage by creating more interests and broadening the range of sources for joy.

This explains why for a lot of couples, the mood right after the wedding ceremony could be described as, "Let the disappointment begin!" It happens all the time. Even the honeymoon may fall flat, especially if you were sexually active before the marriage. In addition, all the tensions that are pent up in the last days of the engagement—things you thrust aside so they won't tarnish the buildup to the big day—tend to come flowing out after the wedding. As time goes on more unmet expectations accumulate. You hone in on each other's weaknesses. You bear down on each other's faults. And if that is all you do, it's no wonder you can end up with so much disconnection early on.

That is why friendship, laughter, humor, "sporting," and doing things you enjoy is so important. You can sulk about your sorry situation or you can decide to get active, doing things you both enjoy that may trigger a revitalizing laugh or two.

In some cultures, past and present, husbands and wives don't generally seem to be friends. Marriages in many times and places were and still are arranged by parents, and sometimes the bride and groom don't meet each other until their wedding day. I love the classic musical *Fiddler on the Roof*, but the one thing about it that has always disturbed me a little is that Tevye and Golda, though married twenty-five years and having five daughters together, don't seem to be good friends. They continually bicker and frustrate each other. Finally in the song "Do You Love Me?" they come to realize they love each other, but I never get any hint that their love involves friendship. And that is very sad and very typical of many marriages.

If you have read any of my other books, you are aware that I have opened up about some huge blunders I have made in my life. So I feel that on the rare occasions when I do something right, I have earned the right to tout it a bit. This morning I made a major decision to be a friend to my wife. I was rushing about because I needed to get out the door and on an airplane. But she was looking a little down, as if she needed a friend. I didn't know if her sadness was over the recent loss of her father or something related to the kids. So I went over and hugged her and asked what she needed. She wanted to take a walk with me. So I changed my airport clothes and we went out for a walk.

It wasn't a long walk, but long enough for her to rebuild her feelings of connection and friendship with me and to help her face certain challenges before her. We talked about some tough decisions we needed to make and assured each other we were on the same page and moving in the same direction. I told her she is the best thing I have going and the person I love. We held hands, talked, and returned twenty minutes later a stronger couple just because we took a few minutes to be friends.

Friendship forms the foundation for the fun and humor that make marriage enjoyable at times and endurable at others.

Friendship forms the foundation for the fun and humor that make marriage enjoyable at times and endurable at others. Marriage without friendship may work in some cultures, but not in our culture. If husbands and wives don't nurture their friendship, their marriage can fizzle into a kind of business relationship where daily responsibilities of career and children drain the emotional connection. According to marriage counselor and pastor Bill Hanawalt, "Couples that don't give attention to developing their friendship often come apart. It also creates an opening for marital infidelity."[1]

Everybody needs friends. Having same-sex friends outside of marriage can actually build the friendship you have with your mate. The reason is simple. Friends can help encourage you through tough spots. They can meet some needs—especially those benefiting from the viewpoint of your own sex—that your mate might not meet as effectively. They can help you see things from a different perspective.

Both husband and wife benefit from time spent with friends of their own sex where they can indulge certain interests exclusive to their particular sex. With their buddies, men can talk freely about their toys and sports without boring their women to tears. With other women, wives can talk of, well, just about everything, especially the things in which even the best of husbands can hardly pretend an interest.

Same-sex friendships can help the marriage not only in this way, but also by broadening the scope of experience each mate brings into the marriage. You can overdo time spent with other friends, but maintaining reasonable connections with them can really help you have a more satisfying marriage. The problems with same-sex friendships emerge when the spouse invests more emotional capital in the outside friendship than in friendship with his or her mate.

FRIENDS ENJOY THINGS TOGETHER

A primary characteristic of friendship is doing together the things you both like to do. When you were dating you discovered you had common interests, and those were the things you did together. This is surely one reason—aside from your irresistible sexual magnetism, of course—that you were attracted to each other. So, the question is, do the two of you still do any of those things you did when you were dating? If not, have you replaced them with fun things more suitable to your age or physical abilities? Or, like so many married couples, have you allowed fun to fade into the background or even disappear in the clutter of cares, responsibilities, humdrum routines, or the so-called realities of life?

I have heard some couples complain that over the years they have grown apart, and they no longer have in common those things that first drew them together. Well, I agree that we all grow and change as we mature. When people marry young, as the majority of couples do, these changes may be dramatic, as both are still discovering themselves and defining who they are. This can mean diverging interests, but it need not mean the couple drifts apart. Even if you develop widely different interests, each of you can make it a point to show interest in the other's pursuits. And you can maintain a firm grip on those things in common that initially drew you together.

I think a lot of couples would enjoy each other if they were more like Alan and Judy. When Alan and Judy married, they had all kinds of things in common. Both loved Broadway musicals, gospel music, historical movies, badminton, and travel. They also had differences. He was a great reader and loved to talk about books, philosophy, and religion. She, on the other hand, loved to spend her time working in the yard (which was drudgery to him). She read little and had no interest in intellectual discussion.

In time Alan wrote more than a dozen books, which were all published, and he was called to speak in various forums and lecture at universities. Judy made an attempt to read his first few books out of sheer loyalty, but she got little out of them. And when their children started arriving, she never got around to reading the rest.

You might think that such a divergence in interests would damage their marriage, or at least cool it considerably. But it did not, because both Alan and Judy focused on their common interests and shared them regularly. They traveled and antiqued together, watched and discussed historical movies, attended gospel music concerts, maintained an active church life and Bible study, focused on raising their children, and kept in close contact with them when they grew up and had children of their own.

Furthermore, they maintained a sense of fun. Sometimes as they moseyed through a shopping mall, Alan would start belting out the song he heard played over the mall's music system, causing Judy to duck her head and veer into the nearest store. If Alan ventured out into the yard when Judy was watering flowers, it most likely meant a water fight.

No one can be alike in every way, but everyone can focus on the important things they have in common and share those activities to the fullest. Though Judy doesn't read Alan's books and Alan barely knows a petunia from a dandelion, they have remained best friends through more than fifty years of marriage. Maybe you have stopped thinking this way and living like this. Maybe you need some new additions to your repertoire of behaviors. Choosing new things to do could spark a fire in your marriage.

ACTIVE FUN INCREASES INTIMACY

One of the biggest complaints I hear in marriage is a lack of sexual intimacy. The bottom line is that activity and exertion outside the bedroom often lead to more sexual activity in the bedroom. I have done a couple of book projects with Bill and Pam Farrel. In their book *Red-Hot Monogamy*, they tell us that couples increase intimacy when they engage together in fun activities that involve bodily exertion.[2] Instead of letting your dates get stuck in the rut of going out to eat and to the movies, plan dates that involve physical activity of some kind.

Bodily activity produces endorphins—the "happy chemical." We know that physical activity increases physical health and, according to James White, PhD, "Research suggests that people who get regular aerobic exercise have more sex, better orgasms . . . than non-aerobic exercisers."[3]

Another benefit of engaging in physical activity together is that it increases relational health by strengthening the bond of friendship between married lovers. I don't know whether the better sex is due to the increased bodily health or the increased bond of togetherness—but who cares?

If you have trouble thinking of recreational activities for the two of you to enjoy, Bill and Pam provide an excellent list in their article, "Recreational Intimacy" on the Focus on the Family website.[4]

THE POWER OF FUN AND LAUGHTER

One of the iconic women's movies of the current generation is *Steel Magnolias*. In this film, M'Lynn Eatenton (Sally Field) loses her daughter to kidney disease. After the funeral she and her small group of women friends are at the cemetery when she breaks down in grief and anger, crying and ranting at the unfairness of her daughter's early death. She says she is so angry she just wants to hit someone.

The friends gape in appalled silence at their dear friend's distress until one of them, Clairee, grabs the sour character Ouiser and thrusts her forward, saying, "Here, hit Ouiser!" The grieving mother stops her tirade in surprise and then bursts into uncontrolled laughter.

You would hardly think it possible to find the funniest moment in a story at the point of its deepest tragedy, but that is the power of humor. Laughter can defuse tension, turn a bad situation into good, or lift a person's spirits when he or she is dragging. According to humorist Arnold Glasow, "Laughter is a medicine with no side effects." And it's a medicine every married couple should take in regular doses.

In one family the young children heard strange noises coming from their living room. They ran in to see their mother in an apron with their father holding her about the waist as he nuzzled her neck, causing her to giggle and squeal as she squirmed to get away. (I believe they were *sporting*!) As the children watched in fascination, their parents lost their balance and fell to the sofa, breaking its frame with a resounding crack. Ruining the sofa was worth the lesson in playful love the children witnessed in their parents. Though they are now grown, those kids still enjoy telling this story.

I urge a little caution here: sometimes couples (especially guys) think that teasing and playing jokes on each other is fun. In some cases perhaps it could be if done with careful sensitivity. But most of the time I have found that such jokes tend to be hurtful and disconnecting. I suspect that partners resort to this kind of humor when they don't know how to connect in more intimate ways. If you are a couple who happens to enjoy playing jokes on each other, the basic rule that should never be violated is to be sure everything you do causes you to laugh *with* and not *at* your mate. The joke or trick must be mutually enjoyable, and never should one mate be the butt of the other's laughter. This also means, of course, that in telling a joke or funny story about your mate in public, you never make him or her the butt of the joke or the object of ridicule. Never!

I believe you should avoid practical jokes completely. Almost all practical jokes are funny only to the one playing them, not to the victim. Never, ever play a cruel joke on your mate (or anyone else). I've seen a few video clips of people reacting to faked winning lottery tickets given as a joke. Those "jokes" do the opposite of what humor should do. They cause high elation and then bring the person down to extreme disappointment. Why would anyone think that is funny? Humor should do the opposite and lift one from negative to positive emotions.

Never play jokes that could result in pain or injury. This includes even the use of fake snakes, rats, or spiders. Some people have irrational phobias of such creatures, and their panic to get away could cause falls or collisions with objects that would result in injury. The principle, again, is to do things where you can laugh *with*, not *at* your mate.

On second thought, I believe we might make one exception to the "laugh with and not at" rule. It occurs sometimes when the other does something inadvertently that is truly funny. What if you're in church and your mate falls asleep, and when his head falls forward he suddenly snorts and jerks upright? Yes, your mate is embarrassed. Yes, according to the humor rule, you shouldn't laugh. But the question is, how can you keep from chuckling? Especially in church where anything funny is ten times funnier.

The answer, I think, is to learn to laugh at yourself. All of us should learn not to take ourselves too seriously and be quick to laugh at our own inevitable foibles. You know that sometimes you inadvertently do things your spouse can't help but see as funny. When that happens, the best way to respond is to join in the fun and laugh at yourself. Where's the fun in taking yourself seriously?

In closing this chapter it's noteworthy to observe that the "sporting" Isaac and Rebekah must have been just the kind of couple that in this chapter I've been urging married people to become. We think of those Old Testament patriarchs as too staid, upright, and dignified to have fun. Not Isaac!

And apparently not Rebekah either. Some women are too reserved or sophisticated to play and have fun. But I see Rebekah as a woman who giggled and ran when she was tickled, but only fast enough to get caught and find great joy in losing the race and the playful wrestling match that likely followed.

As the wise King Solomon might have said, now that all has been heard, here is the conclusion of the whole matter: the couple that plays together, stays together.

THINGS TO DO
TO HAVE FUN WITH YOUR SPOUSE

——⬤——

- Make plans to share a fun, even silly activity with your spouse. Get outside your routine and let yourself relax and really enjoy each other for a while.

- Sit down with your spouse and make a list of five things you both love to do or used to do and agree you are going to schedule them over the next couple of months.

- If finances are a concern, start saving for whatever you can afford even if all you can afford to do initially is rent some old movies you saw together and loved.

- Be willing to sacrifice spending money on something you enjoy as an individual, so you can spend that money on both of you having some fun.

- If your spouse loves to do certain things that you hate to do, be willing to participate in those things and see if that does not open the door to him or her doing some things you love to do.

- If your spouse won't do anything fun, you do some fun and interesting things anyway, inviting your spouse to join you, allowing your mate to see that fun things energize you and positively impact the relationship.

- Plan something with another couple and if you have no couples in your life, fix that problem on the way to addressing this one.

- Since mutual vulnerability will draw you closer, do some things neither of you do well and both of you are a little or a lot uneasy with such as skydiving, mountain climbing, scuba diving, or anything that might cause you to hold onto each other a little tighter while you are having fun together.

- Don't allow yourself to become addicted to sameness, predictability and safety. Willingness to try something new will produce a greater strength in every area of your relationship.

- If you can't think of anything fun or new or exciting or challenging for the two of you to fully engage in or just to try one time, consult a friend, a pastor or counselor and ask them to give you their best ideas to create fun and friendship.

2

———◯◯———

Respond Romantically to Your Mate

To watch a short video on this subject, go to
7MinuteMarriageSolution.com/9

When my wife and I got married, we wanted to be sure we understood how to have a sexually wonderful marriage. (Actually she searched online for something to help us, ME, get this part of our relationship right.) So we enrolled in a workshop conducted by a physician couple, and it made all of the difference in the world. We had waited to have sex until we were married, but once married we did not really know how to make it lasting and great. That workshop really helped us in this area.

There was one concept that blared at us throughout the weekend. Sexual satisfaction comes from investing in the other person's joy and pleasure. It does not come from seeking to gratify yourself. You will naturally want what you want, but the only way you will get what you want is to invest in the other person's needs and desires. I know that is not a new concept, but I stress it yet again because we tend to forget it, and it is foundational in developing and maintaining a rewarding and growing life of romance and sexual intimacy.

Sexual satisfaction comes from investing in the other person's joy and pleasure. It does not come from seeking to gratify yourself.

Over the course of a few days I watched struggling couples in the workshop start to glow in each other's eyes as their resentments and irritations were replaced with attention and care. And I have no doubt that the glow is still burning in the lives of those who continue to practice what we learned. It certainly is in our marriage.

For most couples the glow of romance starts with a spark of attraction that builds into a raging fire. It is usually an unforgettable moment. How well Clint remembered that moment. He was dating Karen, the woman who was to become his wife, and they were to meet that evening at a sidewalk restaurant in the arts district. Clint arrived a few minutes early, found a table overlooking the lake, and sat down to wait. Minutes later he saw her, and the vision took his breath away. She was walking toward him with her usual grace, every movement the essence of feminine perfection. The rim of her hair blazed like fire from the setting sun behind her. As she drew closer he could see the velvet surface of her face, flawless and glowing. Her blue eyes sparkled like diamonds framed by long, curling lashes. When Karen saw Clint, she smiled. It was good that he was sitting down, he thought, or that smile would have buckled his knees. Surely he was beholding a goddess, a creature of ethereal wonder. Simply gazing on her filled his soul with all the ecstasy he could stand.

Clint's thoughts must have been similar to Adam's when he saw the glorious, newly created woman (and might I add, a beautifully naked woman) God had created just for him. He knew immediately that they were made for each other. He said, "'This is now bone of my bones and flesh of my flesh; she shall be called "woman," for she was taken out of man.' That is why a man leaves his father and mother and is united to his wife, and they become one flesh" (Genesis 2:23–24 NIV). The physical design of the man and woman shows that God created them for intimate relationship with each other.

What are we to make of those exquisite sensations, the glow, the excitement, the awe, the palpitations Clint experienced as Karen approached—and I'm sure Adam experienced as Eve approached? What are we to make of this mystery we call romance? What are we to make of the euphoria we feel in the intimacy of the sexual embrace? Everyone who experiences these feelings hopes they will last forever.

We're told, however, that the glory of sex and romance will not last. It is an illusion that fades after the honeymoon as the inevitable reality of humdrum routines settles over the marriage like a dark cloud.

But that is wrong! I know it seems to be right: common experience shows that romance tends to fade. Yet Solomon's magnificent love song gives exquisite evidence that the glory of sexual romance is not an illusion but a solid reality in God's creation. When we call romance a fantasy and the things that destroy it the true reality, we invert the truth. When God created sex, he made romance—that impelling fascination and attraction between the sexes—a reality. Just as Adam and Eve were created to live forever, so was romance. It's true that romance does not tend to last. But this fading occurs not because it's a fantasy but because of the work of our adversary.

In that magical moment when Clint watched Karen approaching, the veil of illusion was lifted. When he saw emanating from her the aura of a goddess, he was seeing her exactly as God created woman to be seen. At that moment Clint's vision penetrated the dulling fog we fallen humans live in and he saw true reality—the glory that God built into every woman and man he ever created. God meant for the relationship between husband and wife to be one of lasting joy and wonder.

There are ways to counter Satan's influence and bring back into our marriages the reality of romance. For romantic and sexual intimacy to remain intact, the love that adores the body must reach deeper to enfold the heart. When inevitable cares and troubles assail the marriage and the infirmities of age encroach, a deeply committed love will preserve the magic. It will enable couples to retain their masculine and feminine glory even when youthful desire and beauty wane. Couples whose souls become knit together never fail to experience the glory of romantic intimacy.

God created in each sex a yearning for the other so strong it's as if the heart of each is a magnet reaching out to draw the other into a mystical oneness. Professor Christopher West eloquently describes the power of this mutual longing by incorporating phrases from the Song of Solomon: "God created males and females with a yearning for love that 'burns like a blazing fire, like a vehement flame' that 'many waters cannot quench' and 'rivers cannot wash away.'"[1] He is describing sex and romance. Genesis 2:23–25 also describes sex and romance. God obviously wants us to find ecstasy in sex and romance!

Sex and romance go hand in hand, and both are highly sensual experiences. The sensuality of romance includes that magical aura, the palpitations we feel at the sight or touch of the other, the fascination of every detail about the form and movements of the other. The sexual embrace provides the highest, most ecstatic physical sensations a person can experience. That is the glory of sex and romance, and that is also its Achilles' heel.

DISTRUST OF THE SENSUAL

One of our problems with romance and sex springs from a heritage of Christian distrust of anything sensual. *Sensual, sensuous,* and *sensuality* have been dirty words for Christians in the not-too-distant past. Previous generations seem to have thought those words should have been spelled *sin*sual, *sin*suous, and *sin*suality. Obviously, equating sin with the sensual is an error. *Sensual* simply means "of the senses." Our whole existence is "of the senses." It depends on the sensual, for there is little we know, feel, or experience that doesn't come to us through one or more of our five senses.

When we think rationally we know that the sensual nature of sex does not make it wrong. God created sex. Yet, in spite of what we know, distrust passed to us from our parents and grandparents often casts subtle shadows over our sexual relationships. No doubt this distrust of the sensual is due partly to how easily the enticement of sensual pleasure can lead us astray. But all good things can be abused; that is the essence of sin. The abuse of a good, however, does not invalidate its inherent goodness.

Another reason we run off the rails with sex and romance is more experiential. Both men and women tend to separate romance from sex, whereas the two are meant to intertwine. To complicate the problem, men tend to separate sex and romance in one way and women in the opposite way. Men tend to emphasize sex and downplay romance; women tend to emphasize romance and downplay sex. I don't mean totally, of course: men enjoy romance and women enjoy sex. But the emphases of men and women tend toward opposite ends of the sex/romance spectrum.

You might think this dual emphasis should work out pretty well. Women need men for romance; men need women for sex; so each has an asset to barter. Men give romance to get sex, and women give sex to get romance. That might all be well and good if you think of the relationship between husband and wife as a commercial transaction. But when it takes that form, each spouse is in the business of getting his or her own needs met, using the spouse as an instrument for that purpose. The emphasis is on the self instead of the other.

A SHIFT IN FOCUS

We all know that it's better to give than to receive (Acts 20:35). Most people assume that means giving is better for us spiritually because it involves sacrifice. But giving offers an even greater benefit, especially when it comes to sex. In giving pleasure you receive more pleasure. Try to get sexual pleasure and you merely experience a temporary physical sensation, which eventually becomes stale and meaningless by repetition. That is why men and women who sleep around perpetually seek new thrills by moving on to new partners. They hope variety will counter the inevitable dulling of repetitive sensation.

The focus of a loving married couple, on the other hand, is not on receiving tingling sensations but on expressing love for the partner. This means that in the sexual embrace, the ecstasy is multiplied because it comes not solely from physical sensation but from the act of giving pleasure to the other. The pleasure is further amplified by the sense of oneness, the experience of shared being, the interplay of personalities, and giving to and receiving from the other exactly what each sex lacks and needs.

This is how couples who commit solely to each other avoid the staleness of repetition and find in sex a continually growing bond and deepening intimacy that achieves the true joy God meant the sexes to find in each other.

The apostle Paul tells us that "husbands ought to love their wives as their own bodies. He who loves his wife loves himself. After all, no one ever hated their own body, but they feed and care for their body" (Ephesians 5:28–29 NIV). If you love your wife's body as you love your own, you will focus on giving her all the pleasure you can. Forget great sex and focus on her, and you stand a better chance of having great sex. When she forgets romance and focuses on him, she stands a better chance of experiencing real romance.

In another passage, Paul makes this principle of husbands and wives giving to each other explicitly sexual. Notice how the focus is entirely on how both married partners should dedicate themselves to the needs of the other. There is no hint here of using sex to achieve one's own satisfaction. Nada. His body belongs to her, and hers to him. It's all about giving one's self to the other, which is the foundational principle of sex and romance in marriage (1 Corinthians 7:3–5).

ROMANCE 101 FOR MEN

Okay, men, now that we have established the basic principle of mutual giving, let's get down to some really practical stuff. Since women crave romance and men have somehow acquired a reputation for being romantically challenged, let's spend a moment looking at what we can do about that little problem.

Here is the key: we tend to make the same mistake in romance that many people make in religion. We know that for a person who truly loves God, worship is not just a Sunday-only thing; it's a way of life. It means being continually God-conscious and pleasing him in all your relationships, activities, transactions, and recreations.

Your relationship with your wife should work in exactly the same way. Romance is not something you do only on romantic occasions; it must be a way of life. It's the way you conduct yourself in your relationship with your wife. You can't spend all week being a slob, neglecting her, ignoring her needs, spending time away from her, and then on Friday night suddenly turn on the charm and wine her and dine her with the intent of getting her to turn on to you when you turn out the light.

One song in Gershwin's great folk opera *Porgy and Bess* is "A Woman is a Sometime Thing." It's a lyrical way of saying that the moods and desires of a woman change dramatically. Maybe she's a sometime thing sexually because you are a sometime thing romantically. Romance can't be just a sometime thing that you turn on when your libido is revving in high gear. It has got to be woven into the essence of your entire relationship with her.

What really fuels romance in a marriage is for each mate to put the other first and be continually attentive to the other's needs.

Don't worry, I'm not about to recommend sending flowers or a card every day or taking her on dates twice every week. These romantic perks are merely the icing on the cake—not the cake itself. They are good and needed on occasion, but they are not the essence of romance. What really fuels romance in a marriage is for each mate to put the other first and be continually attentive to the other's needs.

This means being your wife's companion and friend, putting her first as the one you really want to be with. It means being her confidante, the one with whom you share your deepest secrets, hopes, and desires, and the one in whom she confides without fear of betrayal or judgment. It means caring for her well-being, watching that she is not overworked and attending to her health. It means being thoughtful, kind, and patient with her. It means helping when she needs help, caring for her when she's sick, cheering her up when she's down, laughing with her when she's happy, and exulting in her accomplishments. It means observing the common courtesies of opening doors and seating her at tables. I could go on, but I hope you get the idea.

You may not see these attentions as romance, but believe me, she will. Because if you do all these things, they add up to show that you cherish her, that she is important to you. What makes her melt in your arms is not the flowers or the chocolates; it's becoming a man she admires, respects, looks up to, and depends on. This is what builds a solid foundation of true romance.

Now men, please notice: I said these acts of care you perform for your wife are the *foundation* of romance. They make the cake I spoke of above. But don't get the idea that you can ignore the icing—the flowers, chocolates, cards, and candlelight dinners—or whatever it takes to speak the romantic love language of your spouse. It is crucial that you don't forget birthdays, anniversaries, Valentine's Day, or Mother's Day. That's basic. But it enhances romance when you give her flowers, cards, or take her out on occasions that are not special. She expects you to remember the special days, but when you remember her at other times it makes her feel special for who she is, not just because you did your husbandly duty on a holiday.

And by all means, tell your wife how much you love her. Like voting in a Chicago election, you should do it early and do it often. You may assume your wife knows how much you love her, but hearing you say the words is like Godiva chocolates to her soul. I suppose it's remotely possible that you could say it too often, but with most men that's about as likely as getting hit by a falling meteor.

Yes, I know you're a mighty hunter and a macho honcho, and romancing isn't your cup of tea—uh, I mean mug of grog. To that I have two answers. First, romance is not as unmanly as you think. Masculine clunkyness in romance is something of a modern thing. In the 1700s, 1800s, and early 1900s, educated men in the better parts of society prided themselves on their romantic abilities. It was also part of court life among knights of the Middle Ages. In almost any movie of those periods you will see men dancing, singing in drawing rooms, playing parlor games with women, quoting poetry, writing florid letters, and dressing to the hilt. Even as late as World War I, the most popular reading among British soldiers in the trenches of France was Jane Austen's novels. Men do have a historical romantic streak in them. It may now be latent, but it's there.

My second answer to your resistance to romance is that you can learn to do it. We males are not so dense that we can't learn new tricks. And if we expect to live successfully with a woman, we've got to learn everything we can about them. We're not living in some remote Amazon jungle tribe where the men smoke their reed pipes in the all-masculine security of their own collective hut. We have chosen to share a house with a female, which means the atmosphere percolates as much with estrogen as testosterone. We must adapt ourselves to breathing it. It won't hurt you to switch from ESPN, pop a bowl of popcorn, and watch a few chick flicks with her.

BECOMING ONE WITH YOUR SPOUSE

Eva loved to go "antiquing," but her husband, Matt, hated it. He couldn't see the point of spending a Saturday traipsing through endless rows of dusty junk in one shop after another, looking for nothing in particular. Eva went by herself a time or two, but soon she quit going at all. Matt felt bad about her giving up something she so enjoyed, because he knew it was simply because she didn't like spending that much weekend time away from him.

So one Saturday morning he got up, brewed the coffee, and brought a cup to the bed. "Get up, Eva," he said, handing her the cup of steaming coffee. "We're going to spend the day antiquing." She survived the shock, got ready, and that day they hit every antique mall in two counties. Eva was excited and bubbly the whole day, often taking his hand or squeezing his arm. When they lunched at one of the mall's froufrou restaurants, he was struck by the soul-melting softness of her gaze across the table. *She really loves this*, he thought. *It was worth it.* And that night after they got home and into bed, he found that it was *definitely* worth it!

Guys, if you make this adaptation to the mysterious world of femininity, I'm pretty sure you will like the result.

Something will always be missing in your marriage if the only time you want to be "one flesh" with your spouse is when you crawl into bed at night.

That will show her you are not truly one with her in every way. You are simply using her as an instrument to achieve sensations in your genitals. If that's all you want from marriage, I feel sorry for you, because you are missing out on one of the greatest gifts that God has given man—the incredible joy of being truly one with a woman in every way. When that oneness includes love and romance—by which I mean all the mental, emotional, and relational connections I noted above—the sexual act becomes not merely a matter of genital friction but an ecstatic oneness that permeates the entire bodies and souls of both persons. You don't want to miss out on this wonderful, God-given gift. The Bible makes it clear that sex is a gift God means for a married couple to enjoy. As Proverbs 5:18–19 says, "Let your fountain be blessed, and rejoice with the wife of your youth. As a loving deer and a graceful doe, let her breasts satisfy you at all times; and always be enraptured with her love" (NKJV).

Your wife won't welcome your penis into her body until your love has entered her heart to prepare the way. That leads to my most famous equation: erection minus connection equals rejection. It's not easy to argue with that, is it? It means building and maintaining that foundation of romance. If, from a sense of duty, she lets you enter her body sexually when you have not entered her heart emotionally, she will see it as a selfish intrusion, and she will build up resentment and resistance to your sexual advances. If she often has a headache, consider the possibility that you are putting your own sexual wants ahead of your care for her. Putting her first may cure those headaches faster than any aspirin. Keep it up and she may start dragging you to the bedroom.

SEX 101 FOR WOMEN

Women, you have probably already learned that your husband's sexual desire is hair-triggered, ready to fire at the slightest pressure. But a woman's sexual desire is seldom as pressing or obvious. More buttons have to be pushed and more switches flipped to release the firing mechanism. That doesn't mean your desire is less than his—both men and women love sex—but in you it is generally planted deeper, and it must be drawn out. For this reason, most women don't share the strong urgency for sex that men feel, and this is one of the sources of frustration between married couples.

I urge you not to allow this tension to cause you to abandon hope of sexual pleasure. Don't push sex to the side or allow your sexuality to go dormant. Don't fall into the easy habit of letting him have his sex on your disengaged body. That will build up resentment on your part and dissatisfaction on his.

One way to resolve the tension of differing levels of desire is for you to allow him to draw out your sexual desire through foreplay—to bring you up to the point where your desire matches his. You may go to bed thinking you have no desire for sex tonight, when in fact it may be there but too far beneath the surface to be recognized. It's possible that if you allow your husband to draw it out, your desire may soon match his.

It's also possible—in fact, I think it's probable—that he may not at first know how to do this. Many women seem to think men have built-in instincts enabling them to know how to please a woman sexually. Unfortunately, men seem to think it, too, because over the years I have heard so many women complain that their men are sexually confident but utterly incompetent. They think they know how to satisfy a woman, but they end up satisfying only themselves. The complaint I hear most often is, "It's all about him. He doesn't care what I want or what works for me."

That complaint doesn't necessarily mean the husband is "being intentionally self-focused; he simply needs to learn something he thinks he knows but doesn't. Men do not automatically know how to satisfy a woman sexually. It's a learned skill. While your husband may learn much before marriage through reading or advice, he cannot know exactly what pleases you personally. Every woman is different in terms of what arouses her and what doesn't. You must be your husband's teacher. Communicate to him your sexual needs. Let him know what works and what doesn't.

Many women feel reticent about talking of such things. If that's your problem, I urge you to overcome it. Think of it as a way of sharing a deep intimacy with your husband. It's something that only you and he know, that only you and he can discuss, that only the two of you can learn by experimentation. It helps to remember that sexual pleasure is God's design. Talking about it with the man he gave you to provide that pleasure is perfectly acceptable, and it can even be enjoyable.

While men tend to be sexually confident even when they have little reason to be, women tend to lack sexual confidence even when they have good reason to possess it. Usually a woman's lack of sexual confidence involves body issues. Because of today's impossible standards for female beauty, few women think their bodies measure up to the air-brushed models they see in the media.

This was Valerie's problem. She was about fifteen pounds over the "ideal" (whatever that means) weight for her height. On her wedding night, she was too embarrassed to let her husband see her naked, so she undressed and slipped under the covers before he came out of the bathroom. But when she gave in to his pleading and reluctantly uncovered, she could tell by the light of excitement in his eyes and the tremor of his voice when he whispered, "Wow!" that the sight of her body was a real feast for him. She never worried about her body again.

It would help women to know that the ideal set by media models is a rarely achieved, virtually impossible standard. It should help even more to realize that few men like this standard as well as people assume. What men like in the female body is all over the board, from heavy to thin, tall to short, hippy to slender, big-breasted to small-breasted. To see the truth of this, take a brief excursion into art history and compare Peter Paul Rubens's painting of Eve[2] to that of Lucas Cranach.[3] The two Eves are as different as marshmallows and toothpicks, yet each was the ideal for the artist's time and place.

You may feel insecure about your body because it is augmented or because it is not, because it does not look anything like Barbie or it looks too much like her. But give yourself a break. What turns on almost every man I know is a wife's willingness. So just relax and accept yourself as you are. If you accept yourself and show confidence in your appearance, he will accept it as well.

DOS AND DON'TS FOR
MUTUALLY SATISFYING SEXUALITY

There are not many rules for what a husband and wife should or shouldn't do in the bedroom, but there are a few that should be observed for mutually satisfying sex. Here are some practical suggestions.

Never use sex as a bargaining chip to get something you want from your mate, and never withhold sex as punishment for some offense he or she has committed. This turns sex into a bartering commodity instead of a mutually enjoyable experience that one gives freely to the other.

If your partner doesn't want to do it, don't push.
Always do only what is mutually satisfying and enjoyable.

Never push your mate into sex when it's clearly not wanted. The reason for your spouse's not wanting sex may or may not be valid. It could be physical discomfort, the wrong place, the wrong time, or some mental or emotional distraction involving work or family. It could be some issue between the two of you that first needs to be resolved. When one wants the connection and the other doesn't, sex will not be a mutually enjoyable experience.

Never push your mate into modes of sex that he or she finds repelling or uncomfortable. Variety and experimentation are fine when they don't involve harm, perversion, humiliation, or risk to health. But if your partner doesn't want to do it, don't push. Always do only what is mutually satisfying and enjoyable.

Again I urge women to tell their husbands what works for them and what doesn't. Husbands, if she doesn't tell you, then make it a point to ask. Learn your mate's sexual response triggers. If she cannot overcome her reticence to tell you, then learn what you can about women's sexual responses in books or talk to your pastor or counselor. And this works the other way as well. Wives need to know what turns their husbands on and, for practical reasons, also what slows him down so he won't peak before you are ready.

Let him tell you what works and what doesn't as the two of you experiment and learn through practice.

Finally, don't expect the same experience in every sexual encounter. Intensity waxes and wanes. Moods change, depending on what the day or week has been like. Sometimes sex may be deep, slow, and romantic. At other times it may be frenzied and urgent. At yet other times it may be playful and accompanied by lightheartedness and laughter. The key to satisfying sex is for both of you to learn to expect nothing but to enjoy what is given.

THINGS TO DO
TO ENSURE YOU AND YOUR SPOUSE
HAVE GREAT SEX

———◯◯———

- Tend to each other's needs outside the bedroom. Initiate romance early in the day and maintain that all day long.

- Eliminate interference when you have times of intimacy together.

- Continue to remind each other of the good things about each other and the relationship.

- Try new things together. Never push your partner to do something they don't want to do, but be open to new experiences and explore new ways to please each other.

- Any man involved with pornography or any other form of sexual betrayal of his spouse must find what resource will help him stop, stop and start building character that was eroded by betrayal of trust. (wedared.com, *Every Man's Battle* by Fred Stoeker and Stephen Arterburn, The Every Man's Battle Workshop at 800NewLife.)

- Any woman who criticizes, controls, or compares her man is neutering him and creating a little boy. She becomes the mother to a male child. Intimacy is destroyed. Instead, nurture the little boy inside and call out the man. If he needs help, demand that he get it. If you need help, you reach out and get help.

- Grace builds connection at all levels. Shame kills it. Help each other out of shame and stepping into a life of God's grace.

3

---⊙---

Express Grace and Forgiveness

To watch a short video on this subject, go to
7MinuteMarriageSolution.com/10

Forgiveness within marriage is an act that binds two people together in the midst of their failures and in spite of their imperfections. Without forgiveness, there is no hope for a couple to have a good or godly marriage. Forgiveness can be painful, and sometimes it seems almost impossible. But with God's help it can be accomplished at the right time and in the right way. When forgiveness occurs, the whole relationship is transformed. When it is not there, relational deterioration can be fast and furious and lasting.

What I am about to share is not self-serving. It will not result in any benefit to me financially or otherwise. But it could change everything for you. I recently had the pleasure of working with a couple who had been divorced for two years. Why? Could not forgive. The grace they needed to provide each other was beyond their capacity to develop on their own.

If you have ever read anything I have written, I think you will find a common theme that I do not believe in quick fixes or instant solutions. But there is a solution that can turn things around very quickly as it did in the lives of this couple bitterly divorced for two years. It is called The Marriage Solution Weekend. That is what we created at New Life to help marriages. It is a weekend intensive with great content and Christian counselors to lead small groups.

There is no one-size-fits-all way to deal with specific past hurts. The nature of the hurt and its effect on your present relationship dictates how it should be handled.

The couple attended and two years of bitterness was resolved in two days. They remarried the day before Easter 2015. Couples so bitter they have had restraining orders against each other have come, stayed in separate rooms and found healing, and then a new marriage. Others have brought a troubled marriage and watched the troubles transform into battles to win together. If you cannot create forgiveness in your heart so you can express it, do something that will lead to forgiveness and acceptance of your spouse or even your ex spouse.

There is no one-size-fits-all way to deal with specific past hurts. The nature of the hurt and its effect on your present relationship dictates how it should be handled. But there is one necessary component to healing no matter what kind of hurt you are dealing with, and that is forgiveness. Nowhere is forgiveness more needed than in marriage. You may be the most perfect husband since Adam or the winner of the wife-of-the-year award, but you can be sure that you have done things and will do things that hurt your mate. It's as certain as dogs chase cats. And that hurt can erect a wall between the two of you that can be torn down only by forgiveness. Failure to forgive reinforces the wall, blocking marital harmony and preventing closeness. Each unresolved conflict or unforgiven hurt adds a brick to the wall and prolongs your emotional separation.

I am convinced that forgiveness benefits the forgiver more than the forgiven. If you nurse a hurt or hold on to it with resentment, anger, or thoughts of revenge, it's like swallowing acid. It will eat at you until it destroys you from the inside. Bitterness will undermine your happiness, your marriage, and your physical health. When you forgive, you put away all thoughts of retribution or revenge.

As mentioned earlier, the first step in dealing with hurts in a marriage is to develop sensitivity to your mate's hurts and learn to understand your own. This means delving into the cause of the hurt and the impact it has had. This commitment to understanding enables you to separate the problem from the person, which allows you to hate and attack the problem without hating or attacking the person. You learn to see your mate's hurtful actions not as personal attacks, but for what they are—the spill-off from an overflow of pain. This more accurate viewpoint makes it much easier to take the second step, which is to forgive.

Separating the sin from the sinner was what Jesus did for the Samaritan woman at the well in John 4. This woman felt too shamed by her sins to mix with decent women who drew their water at the communal well in the cool of the morning. She slipped out in the heat of the day to avoid their snubs and stares. But Jesus knew the cause of her pain. Before living with her present partner, she'd had five husbands and suffered five heartbreaking rejections. Jesus understood her past, loved her in spite of it, and forgave her.

In this incident Jesus models to us how we should treat all erring people, and that must apply especially to our own mates. As the apostle Paul tells us, "As God's chosen people, holy and dearly loved, clothe yourselves with compassion, kindness, humility, gentleness and patience. Bear with each other and forgive one another if any of you has a grievance against some-one. Forgive as the Lord forgave you. And over all these virtues put on love, which binds them all together in perfect unity" (Colossians 3:12–14 NIV).

ARE THERE LIMITATIONS TO FORGIVENESS?

What should you do when you forgive your mate for an offense against you, and then he turns right around and does the same thing again? This question has apparently puzzled people since Bible times, because in Matthew 18 we read of the apostle Peter asking Jesus, "Lord, how many times shall I forgive my brother or sister who sins against me? Up to seven times?" Peter obviously thought seven consecutive forgivings would be quite generous. If my wife kept on committing the same offense, forgiving her seven times seems overly generous to me. But it didn't to Jesus. He answered Peter, "I tell you, not seven times, but seventy-seven times" (vv. 21–22 NIV).

Whoa! That's really a test of patience, Lord. I guess that means I've got to bite my tongue, hold my temper, and keep forgiving my wife until that seventy-eighth offense, and then I can finally let the hammer down. Right? Wrong! What Jesus actually meant was that there are no limits on forgiveness. Come to think of it, that's a very good thing. Instead of thinking how irksome it is to have to forgive someone over and over, I need to think about how many times I sin against God. Suddenly I become eternally thankful that he forgives over and over again. What I must not forget is that I should be more than willing to pass on that same forgiveness to others—especially to my mate. In a relationship as close as marriage, forgiveness is a continuing need. Both you and your mate must freely exercise it often.

THE DIFFERENCE BETWEEN
FORGIVING AND ALLOWING

But while there are no limitations to the principle of forgiveness, that does not mean any behavior is to be tolerated. Let's explore the difference between forgiving and allowing.

If a man is married to an alcoholic wife, he may think that forgiving her of this behavior means accepting it and just learning to live with it. That is not the case at all. You forgive her because you realize that you are not her judge. That is, you do not condemn her for her behavior or hold it against her as resentment in your own heart. If you have gone through the process of understanding her, you will even empathize with the pain that led her into drinking. But if you allow the behavior to continue, you are doing great harm to her and to your marriage. To forgive and allow destructive behavior to continue is not the way of love. It's called enabling, or codependence.

If a you are married to a physically or emotionally abusive person, the same principle applies. You can forgive the person, but you must not accept the behavior or allow it to continue because it can cause great harm to you and your children. It is imperative that when addictions or abuse are involved, steps must be taken to stop the behavior. This may include treatment and joining a twelve-step Life Recovery group or program. If these options are refused, there must be consequences to the behavior. In most cases, it's best that the two separate until the problem is thoroughly resolved.

Note that Jesus did not accept the immoral behavior of the Samaritan woman. He addressed it head-on and dealt with it. That is why you should never "forgive and forget." Forgive, yes; but to forget—if such a thing were even possible—would be foolish. Forgetting would set you up to be victimized again. To forget or to act like you forget means there are no consequences to the offending behavior. It signals that the offending spouse is not required to make any change. On the other hand, forgiving and not forgetting motivates the couple to establish new boundaries to prevent recurrence of the offense.

Not forgetting does not mean, however, that when the person is working on resolving the problem that you hold back one iota from complete forgiveness. To be authentic, forgiveness must be total and unreserved. That means, even though you do not forget, you must not in future disagreements throw the offense back into the face of your mate or use it as ammunition. This shows that some residue of resentment remains lodged in your heart. Couples often do this almost unwittingly in arguments by using the terms "you always" and "you never." "You always take your mother's side against me," or "You never do anything I want to do." Terms such as these show that the forgiveness is not complete.

WHY IS IT SO DIFFICULT TO FORGIVE?

Forgiving serious offenses is not easy. If you find that you cannot simply make the decision to forgive and have it happen instantly as if you had waved a magic wand, don't despair or beat yourself up for your spiritual shallowness. Forgiveness is a process that takes time, work, and diligent prayer. But it is worth the effort because you cannot find healing without it.

Forgiveness must be accomplished without accepting or condoning the hurtful behavior.

You may be reluctant to forgive because forgiveness seems too much like an undeserved favor you grant to the offending mate. It seems that you are letting him or her off the hook, as if the offense was of no consequence. That is not the case at all. Forgiveness must be accomplished without accepting or condoning the hurtful behavior. Forgiving without setting boundaries for future behavior and requiring change—and even in appropriate cases, reparation—is a sure setup for repetition of the hurt.

Another reason we are reluctant to forgive is that we find a certain kind of self-justification in holding on to blame. As long as I can blame the other person for what he or she did to me, then I am off the hook. I bear no responsibility for what happened to cause my resentment. I can evade my own sense of guilt by putting it all on that other person who wronged me.

At New Life Ministries, we conduct Women in the Battle weekend workshops for women who have been betrayed by their husbands' lack of sexual integrity. Many of these women were just living their lives and happily living in blissful ignorance until they discovered that their husbands lived in another sexual world they were not aware of. These women are understandably devastated by the horrific revelations that come to the surface. Their anger and grief is often deep, their resentment justified, their brokenness beyond anything they thought they could ever endure.

It is easy for any of these women to fall into the trap of thinking themselves to be all good and the unfaithful husbands all bad. Who wouldn't? It's a natural reaction. But as time and healing occur, these betrayed women must begin to look realistically at their own lives. They did not cause the unfaithfulness, but they were not perfect either. Everyone makes mistakes. The more the betrayed begin to see their own flaws, the more likely they are to be willing to move toward forgiveness and attempt steps that might heal the relationship. This might be the most difficult thing they ever attempt. It also might be the thing that frees them from a life of bitterness, anger, and isolation.

Even when we recognize our sins and deal with them, we often find it hard to forgive ourselves. In fact, this is often one reason we find it so hard to forgive others. Believe it or not, you are the most difficult person you have to forgive. You may try to let go of the guilt and accept God's grace, but your conscience—that often troublesome and legalistic intruder—fails to get the message and continues to prod you, making self-forgiveness a real chore.

Self-forgiveness comes much easier when you realize that God's grace is free and complete. And one of the best ways to know you are forgiven is to forgive others. In forgiving others you can see the forgiveness of God more clearly, simply because you become an enactor and reflector of it. God's character flows through you. Modeling his grace and forgiveness allows you to see the process from the inside and understand up close and personal what God has done for you.

SEEKING FORGIVENESS THROUGH CONFESSION

If you are the spouse who has committed an offense, then your role in restoring the relationship is to seek forgiveness. It is important that you feel true remorse and contrition for the pain you have caused and that you convey those feelings clearly to your mate. You must be willing to make a commitment to him or her that you will not repeat the hurtful behavior. If there are consequences to be borne as a result of the behavior, be ready and willing to bear them, whatever the cost. If your mate has trouble forgiving you, be patient. Remember that forgiveness often takes time, and the deeper the hurt, the more time it may take. In fact, forgiveness may not come until you have taken positive steps to rebuild trust.

Many times the missing element in receiving forgiveness is restitution. It is one thing for a gambling addict to come home and say, "Honey, I lost my job and I gambled away all of our retirement. Will you please forgive me?" It's quite another for him to make restitution: "I can't tell you how sorry I am for all I've done. I pledge to you that I will join Gamblers Anonymous and attend regularly. Tomorrow I promise to get up, put on my coat and tie, and start looking for work. If I must work three jobs, I'll do it. I will put my bass boat up for sale immediately. I'll let you be in charge of the finances from now on. We can go to counseling together and start our healing." An approach such as this is not perfect; confession and restitution doesn't undo the damage or solve all the problems. But if it's sincere, it is the right kind of start in seeking true forgiveness.

When confessing and seeking forgiveness, it is important that you take full responsibility for your own actions. Confessing a wrong and asking forgiveness means expressing remorse, and if your remorse is genuine, you will not justify your action with excuses. If you claim an excusable reason for the hurt you inflicted, then your confession and apology is meaningless. To accompany your apology with an excuse is an illegitimate attempt to justify the hurtful action. You are failing to take full responsibility, putting the blame on another person or on circumstance.

This is why you should avoid "if-but" apologies. They are self-justifying. "I'm sorry *if* I offended you, *but* you need to understand that I was under extreme stress at the time." In other words, it was not really my fault and you should not have been offended because you should understand that I had a valid excuse for doing what I did. "I'm sorry *if* your feelings got hurt, *but* I did not think you would be so sensitive." In other words, it was your fault that my words hurt you, not mine. I was just being myself. You need to develop thicker skin so I won't have to mind my tongue. An "if-but" apology is not really a confession; it's an evasion.

A real confession accepts full responsibility: "I was wrong. I have no excuse for what I did. I was being selfish and did not consider you as I should have. I am very sorry. I promise to make a sincere attempt to do better in the future. Please forgive me."

Related to this principle is the need to be quick to forgive the little things that happen daily in a marriage. We are all fallen creatures who do not always manage our emotions and responses perfectly, and little offenses of no real consequence are sure to be a part of daily life. While you should not blame your offenses against your mate on his or her sensitivity, neither should you let the other's momentary lapse drive a wedge into the relationship. If he is a little snappish when he is struggling to connect a new U-trap under a leaky sink, don't require an apology or a confession. Just let it roll off. He's not upset with you; he's upset with that confounded U-trap or a wrench that keeps slipping or his fumbling hands. Forgive without being asked. If she claims (or has) a headache when you are eager for a romp in the bed, don't pout for the next three days. Forgive her without requiring an apology. Let it roll off. Pouting or complaining is not an effective aphrodisiac likely to make her more eager for the bedroom on the following night.

In a relationship as close as marriage where you are with each other every day for hours at a time, both of you should lower your sensitivity to hurt. Minor everyday failures are sure to happen—a snappish word, forgetting to pick up the cleaning, a failure to compliment a hairdo, overcooking the casserole. Instead of taking offense, be ready to extend grace.

THE CRITICAL IMPORTANCE OF FORGIVENESS

Forgiveness is one of the most critical elements in any relationship. We are all sinners, and we all hurt others. The closer the relationship, the more opportunities for hurt. That is why forgiveness is a key element in binding together a man and woman in marriage.

You should forgive your mate simply because you love him or her. That is why God forgave you, and that alone is reason enough to forgive each other. It will do untold good to your marriage if you and your mate will memorize and practice the plea of the apostle Paul in his letter to the Ephesians: "Be kind to one another, tenderhearted, forgiving one another, even as God in Christ forgave you" (Ephesians 4:32 NKJV).

Choose to forgive your spouse and extend grace to him or her every day. Express an attitude of grace in what you do and how you interact. The more ways you can create to express your attitude of grace, the stronger your marriage will be!

THINGS TO DO
TO EXPRESS GRACE AND FORGIVENESS
———⊙———

- Be sure you have expressed your need to feel your spouse's grace on a daily basis.
- Discuss what things are in the past that both of you have done that are still affecting the relationship today.
- Talk about ways you can meet your spouse's needs in other areas as well as his or her need to feel your grace and acceptance.
- Take responsibility for your mistakes and failures and do whatever it takes for your spouse to know you have.
- Always go beyond saying you are sorry for something that is a repeated offense and be willing to get help if needed.
- If nothing but bitterness seems to come from within, seek the reason why. Explore a lack of forgiveness of yourself or lack of restitution that will enable you to feel forgiven.
- When tempted to criticize, stop yourself, tell yourself you will not hold that against your spouse, then tell your spouse of your love and acceptance.
- If your spouse expresses regret over something from the past, work through any residual resentment and let them know you have forgiven whatever it was.

- To help you express grace, work on your compassion or lack of it for what your spouse has been through and the wounds brought into the marriage.

4

Affirm Your Mate's Strengths

To watch a short video on this subject, go to
7MinuteMarriageSolution.com/11

How much time do you spend criticizing the behavior of your spouse, and how much do you spend affirming his or her strengths? The marriage that makes it is on a journey of acceptance and affirmation. The sooner you get there, the better. Accepting your mate's weaknesses while affirming his or her strengths is one of the requirements of a lasting and meaningful relationship. When you travel toward acceptance and affirmation, you are fleeing from the impossible ideal and into the real. You are discontinuing the rejection of all things that don't meet your expectations. You are offering the grace God has given you to the person you love. You are freed from being disappointed about your spouse's flaws—instead, you are able to identify and appreciate your spouse's good qualities.

Acceptance does more than just liberate you from the disappointment of unmet expectations. It also frees your mate to transform. That's right.

---

*The more you accept the other person,
the more likely it is that your mate will
transform into the best he or she can be.*

The more you accept the other person, the more likely it is that your mate will transform into the best he or she can be. Note that you are not trying to change your spouse. But your acceptance allows your mate the freedom to try new attitudes and behaviors rather than just defend the way he or she has been living. And as you begin to appreciate and affirm your spouse's positive qualities, you free him to cast off some bad habits as he grows into his fullest potential. If you cannot call yourself a person of radical acceptance and affirmation, I invite you to incorporate this liberating concept into your life and into your marriage.

DEALING WITH REAL FLAWS

In all marriages, unsuspected defects, faults, idiosyncrasies, and annoying behaviors show up after the vows are spoken. These flaws vary from trivial to mountainous. Some don't cook well. Some can't hammer any nail but their thumbnail. Some people don't communicate enough. Some communicate too much. Some are not romantic; others are not realistic. Some spend too much; others pinch a penny until it squeals. Some are sloppy; some are neatniks. Some even have serious habits of deceit or secrecy.

Of course, many of our flaws are not merely innocent differences or the result of our gender or background. Instead, they are real faults of varying levels of seriousness. So how should married couples treat these real flaws? There are two answers, depending on what the flaw is. I'll deal first with the most serious problems.

Acceptance does not include abusive, addictive, or other destructive behaviors that require confrontation or intervention. These are behaviors that simply cannot be tolerated. Marital unfaithfulness or physical, mental, or psychological abuse must not be tolerated. Neither should illegal behaviors or addictions like alcohol, drugs, gambling, or pornography.

In a counseling session, one young woman told me what happened when she came out of the bathroom on her wedding night eager to slip into bed with her new husband. He was waiting for her, but to her shock, he was smoking a joint. She stopped immediately, covered herself with a robe, and said, "I never saw you smoking marijuana before, and I am not going to put up with it now. I will not be married to this behavior.

Either you put that thing away and vow never to do it again or I'm walking out of here right now." (I've told this story a lot and it is true and it resonates with a lot of people.) She was unwilling to accept the behavior but willing to accept the person if he separated himself from the behavior.

Committing a serious sin or being caught in an addiction doesn't mean your husband or wife is an all-out bad person—just a person who has made a mistake. The mistake is only one small part of who he or she is. You must not accept the behavior, but you must accept the person who separates himself from the behavior.

DEALING WITH YOUR MATE'S LESSER FAULTS

How should couples deal with the less damaging flaws we have all picked up or acquired in our past—flaws that don't really harm us or our mates, but act as irritants or inconveniences, or cause embarrassment or frustration? The answer: deal with them in the same way you deal with your innocent or inherent differences. Accept them. Maybe he is sloppy, leaving clothes strewn about, not helping with housework, or leaving dishes and glasses wherever he uses them. Maybe she is habitually late, causing you to miss the first minutes of most movies, concerts, and church services. You can probably add a few things to this list yourself.

Running away is the selfish way out. The coward's way. But the way of love, the way of commitment, and the way of Christ is to accept the flaws and weaknesses of your mate and love in spite of them. Let's talk about how this works.

The way of love, the way of commitment, and the way of Christ is to accept the flaws and weaknesses of your mate and love in spite of them.

Marriage is a process of moving out of idealization of the other person to acceptance of all that he or she is and does. The man you married is not the prince you thought he was. The woman you married is not a combination of your mom and a French courtesan. Acceptance involves a process of absorbing this shock of reality and dealing with it. It's actually a process of grieving the loss of the person you thought you married and accepting the reality of the one you did. Every day is an exercise in acceptance. Fortunately in every husband and wife reside great attributes that counterbalance the negatives in the person you accept and love.

THE REWARDS OF AFFIRMATION

You married your mate because you saw great attributes in that person, and you knew you could love someone like that forever. Then you found that along with those lovable attributes came a few unpleasant surprises. What you must realize is that the person you married is a whole package. The desirable and undesirable traits are enmeshed with each other. When you buy the package you accept both the good and the bad; you don't try to remake your mate to fit your own ideal. Instead of focusing on your spouse's flaws by judging or insisting that your mate meet your standards, free your mate to be herself by affirming her strengths. Help your mate to be comfortable in his own skin without having to worry that he's being continually monitored for acceptability.

I believe that deep inside, you want those differences much more than you realize. What you perceive as a flaw likely adds a dimension to your life that you would miss if you married a clone of yourself. Living with someone just like yourself might be more harmonious, but it would also be more boring. How would you experience new perspectives, new ways of thinking, new surprises? Marrying someone who is totally different may bring on more frustrations, but it's also a lot more fun. As the French say, *"Vive la différence!"*

Affirming your mate's strengths does not mean you have to like everything about your mate. That would certainly be a modern-day miracle.

Sometimes she will drive you crazy. Sometimes he will make you want to scream and pull out your hair—or his. But each of you must realize that you also take a lot of putting up with. To receive acceptance and affirmation, you must give acceptance and affirmation. Couples who learn to accept one another as they are find enormous strength for binding their marriage, because it's a marriage built on truth instead of fantasy. This love accepts the flaws but penetrates beyond them and chooses to focus on the positive. Affirming your mate's strengths in spite of his flaws is a sign of mature love.

Affirming your mate's strengths in spite of his flaws is a sign of mature love.

We all have a deep need to have someone who loves us for who we really are. We want someone we can be with without fear of rejection or disapproval. We want someone for whom we don't have to perform in a certain way to earn love. We all want to feel secure that our mate's love is simply there for us and will always be there even when we mess up terribly. We want the kind of love the apostle Paul wrote about when he said, "Love suffers long and is kind; love . . . bears all things, believes all things, hopes all things, endures all things" (1 Corinthians 13:4–7 NKJV). If you will continue to read, I will help you get to that place of love where much is accepted and much is overlooked.

Dr. Jim Bradford, general secretary of the Assemblies of God, tells a story about the "Fault Box." A wife was utterly disgruntled with her husband's abundant flaws and sloppy habits. She had tried to get him to quit leaving his socks strewn about the floor, to quit messing up the kitchen counter with peanut butter, and to correct several other irritating habits. Nothing worked. He persisted in his wayward ways until she decided she had to take more effective steps.

So she set up a box in the kitchen with a slot in the top and labeled it the "Fault Box." She told her husband to write down her faults as he encountered them and drop them into that box. She would do the same, and in thirty days they would open the box and each would read the faults the other had noted.

Over the next thirty days she dropped quite a number of notes into the box. She noticed her husband doing the same. Finally, at the end of the month she called him in, and they sat down to see what each had put in the box. He read the ones she had written first. Each note listed one of his faults—the sloppy habits, the messy counter, and several other failures.

When it was her turn, she unfolded the first note. It said, simply, "I love you." She went to the second note. Same message: "I love you." She went to the third, the fourth, and all the rest. All bore she same message: "I love you." The humbled wife learned something vitally important that day. Each time her husband had noticed one of her faults, instead of listing it he wrote what was more important than the fault itself: his love for her. He covered her faults with his love.[1] It's what the apostle Peter urges us to do: "Above all things have fervent love for one another, for 'love will cover a multitude of sins'" (1 Peter 4:8 NKJV).

It's what we call grace. Just as God in his grace covers our sins with his love, we have the privilege of covering the sins and flaws of our mate with our own love. Marriage gives us a perfect way to become more Christlike—a way of exercising and passing on the same kind of grace he gives to us. It is one more opportunity God gives us to reflect the nature of Christ and to love as he does.

Try to keep this wonderful verse in mind: "Therefore accept each other just as Christ has accepted you so that God will be given glory" (Romans 15:7).

THINGS TO DO
TO AFFIRM YOUR SPOUSE'S STRENGTHS

—⊙—

- To affirm your spouse's strengths you may need to see your spouse for the first time in a positive light, with an accepting heart so those strengths are obvious affirmation points for you to acknowledge.

- If you have difficulty in affirming strength in someone else, it might be due to a weakness in yourself. Examine yourself to see if some work on yourself might increase the affirmation level in your marriage.

- Touch is an affirmation. Provide it liberally.

- Eyeball to eyeball connection affirms all that a person is and builds their confidence in themselves and in the relationship.

- A simple written note comprised of a mention of only one strength costs next to nothing but is more valuable than gold.

- Be sure your eyes are wide open to the strengths of your spouse and half shut to the weaknesses.

- An affirming word to your spouse can be instrumental in changing your attitude into generous affirmation.

5

Spend Money Responsibly

To watch a short video on this subject, go to
7MinuteMarriageSolution.com/12

Boom! That is what I hope you feel from reading this chapter. It is what I felt when I woke up, saw the reality of my financial life, and started making the changes I needed to make. And I was never the same. The boom went off in my head when I realized I had been soothing the bruising of my soul by spending money. Before I married, I had been abandoned and betrayed and I was in pain. The betrayal was so painful I did not know if I would survive or if I wanted to. Spending became my comfort food to numb the pain. Then the depression I was in grew worse because of the debt. I realized I just might die one day and leave my wife in debt. So the extravagant spending stopped, the downsizing started, we attended a financial seminar, and everything everyone had ever said about the freedom of getting out of debt proved true. I hope the boom will go off in your head before it is too late. I hope something in the following pages will explode in front of you, and when the dust clears you will have clarity. Clarity in the area of finances can lead you and your spouse to security and satisfaction that will benefit you for years to come.

Brad and Cheryl, now in midlife and financially comfortable, remember well their first two years of marriage. They were still in college, both working part time earning minimum wage, and money was scarce as icicles in July. Often they ran out of funds before payday. Desperately needing a couple of gallons of gas or a can of beans, they would embark on a quest for cash, scrounging about in furniture drawers, under chairs and sofa cushions and car seats looking for change that might have fallen out of pockets. Or they went on forays along highways picking up aluminum cans and cashing them in.

Today they remember those times fondly. They laugh at the poverty of their early years and claim they lived solely on love. But their memory has done a bit of selective editing. They have forgotten that at the time, their financial struggles were anything but funny.

A lot of couples middle-aged or older are not laughing at the poverty of their younger days because they are still living in those days. They never pulled out of the financial nosedive they faced early in marriage. They find themselves either crashing in financial ruin or barely managing to stay aloft while skimming the crags and treetops, weighted down by heavy debt and out-of-control spending. As a result, money and finances run neck-and-neck with sex as the number-one causes of relational friction in marriage.

Most couples face financial difficulty because they exercise little or no planning or discipline regarding the use of their money. If you want to get out of the stressful cycle of financial strain . . .

- *You may have some tough choices to make.* Save rather than spend. Stay rather than go. Say no rather than yes.

- *You may have some tough habits to break.* Impulse buying. Eating out too often. Relying on plastic. Buying without comparing.

- *You may have some false assumptions to give up.* Everything won't necessarily work according to your financial plan. Faith in God cannot replace financial responsibility. Your investments may not always pay.

- *You may have some acts to surrender or to commit.* Should you surrender the credit cards? Should you commit to a budget? Should the two of you get on the same page financially?

If you are dealing with any of these issues about money, this chapter will give you clarity regarding financial responsibility in your marriage.

COMMON CAUSES OF FINANCIAL CONFLICT

John D. Rockefeller was the first American billionaire. A reporter once asked him, "How much money is enough?" He answered, "Just a little bit more."

That's how we all tend to think, isn't it? *If I had just a little bit more money, a few more things, a little better home, a little newer car, a few more toys, then I would really be happy.* We've heard all our lives that money can't buy happiness, but we don't live like we really believe it. As one wag said, "Money may not buy happiness, but it sure can make unhappiness a lot more comfortable."

Most of us have heard all of our lives that money can't buy happiness. A lot of studies have been done that prove it. But we all think we are the exception or that whether or not it will make us happy, we want as much of it as we can get.

The real problem is their unrealistic expectations, which means they don't have enough money to buy everything they want.

Most couples think just like Mr. Rockefeller. They are convinced their money problems would be solved if they had just a little bit more. That is seldom true. The real problem is their unrealistic expectations, which means they don't have enough money to buy everything they want.

As I write this, the US economy is coming out of a recession and still feels shaky as Jell-O. But people still expect to have all the bells and whistles of comfort, entertainment, and recreation—a large house, fine furniture, seventy-inch HD-TVs in the den and bedroom, a new SUV, motorcycle, ski boat, and cruise vacations. Usually they either buy these things on credit, which causes conflict, or they feel deprived, which causes conflict.

If you tend to spend beyond your income, it may be worth-while to search for the underlying reasons. One common reason is insecurity. You may have been raised in a financially strapped home, and you could not dress as well as your peers or afford the extras they took for granted. Now that you have a little money, you tend to indulge all those things you were previously denied.

You may overspend because you have an unwritten list of accumulated wants that you will buy "when I can afford it." Then when you do get a little extra overtime cash or a tax refund, the entire amount goes to purchasing those wants instead of building a reserve. Spending gives you a rush of freedom from the restraints of having to scrimp.

Many people spend to be like their peers. This is another form of insecurity—a misguided way of saying to others,

"See, I'm just as good as you are. I have value." That is unmitigated pride at work in your life. If you have a problem with uncontrolled overspending, a candid, objective examination of your past or your motives could do much to curb the problem.

Conflict also arises when either spouse spends money secretly. He wants a new hunting rifle. She wants a new dining table. She can't see why he needs another rifle, and he can't see anything wrong with their present table. They don't have the funds for either, so without consulting the other each makes his or her desired purchase. The pattern repeats a few times, money becomes tight, bills go unpaid, and each spouse blames the other for their overstretched budget.

Often the true source of the conflict over finances may not really be about money. One spouse may harbor hurt or resentment in some other area that has not been dealt with. The emotions driven by this deeper hurt may emerge in money disagreements and escalate the conflict to new levels.

My goal in this chapter is simple. I want to help you and your spouse avoid the relational iceberg of financial conflict by getting on the same page financially. I want to help you explore the monetary problems couples tend to have so you can work together to solve them. To this end, I will give you an overview of common wisdom that you can begin applying to your own finances.

YOURS, MINE, OR OURS?

When both the husband and wife earn incomes, the question arises as to who controls the money. In too many homes today, the husband and wife maintain separate bank accounts. I strongly discourage this arrangement because it erodes oneness, leading to separateness in other areas and setting up the couple for power struggles.

While maintaining separate accounts might seem to solve some financial conflict problems by diminishing the need for mutual planning and accountability, it creates other problems. One is inequity. When one income is notably smaller than the other, the spouse with the lesser income may feel like the junior partner in the relationship or suffer a sense of deprivation or inferiority.

Another problem with separate accounts arises when one spouse is financially responsible and the other is not. Chad and Doris were both teachers earning similar incomes. Being a thoroughly postmodern couple, they chose to keep separate bank accounts and share expenses evenly. But Chad had a spending problem, and he consistently blew his paycheck on shop equipment, fishing tackle, golfing, or electronic gadgets. He was usually broke a week before the next check arrived. This meant Doris had to pay most of the bills and pick up the tabs when they ate out, as they typically did during the school year.

You and your mate cannot be truly one as long as you maintain separate finances. Incomes should be merged and managed together. Separate discretionary spending funds within the shared account (a concept I will address below) may sometimes be in order. But that should be the limit of separateness. A shared bank account requires faith and trust in each other. But that is a good thing for your marriage.

PLAN A BUDGET TOGETHER

Many couple's budget problems are due to a failure to communicate to each other their financial priorities. Larry loves to build and repair computers and he's very good at it. He heads up the IT department for a large company, but he has always dreamed of having his own computer repair and consulting business. Every payday he socks away a few dollars toward accomplishing that dream. His wife, Janie, on the other hand, has dreams of redoing her home and yard. Every payday she buys paint, curtains, or shrubs and flowers. When money runs short for bills, both are upset because neither can understand where it all goes.

Like many married couples, Larry and Janie are frustrated because they have never discussed goals that involve the use of money. They have never spoken of budgeting—how to regulate spending to be sure they have money for their goals and needs. The answer is to make it a priority to communicate to each other hopes and expectations that involve money and make a budget that accommodates both necessities and dreams.

Financial matters can get touchy, and it's not uncommon for either mate to be reluctant to discuss them. But there are ways to encourage a husband or wife to do it. Gary Smalley suggests that the wife use word pictures to engage a reluctant husband: "Honey, when you blow off looking at these bills with me and I have to deal with the collectors alone, it makes me feel the same way as I would if I were kidnapped right in front of you and you did nothing to protect me."[1] Ouch! Such a picture is sure to get a caring husband's attention.

Communicate to each other hopes and expectations that involve money and make a budget that accommodates both necessities and dreams.

Christian financial expert Dave Ramsey has advice for persuading a reluctant wife to engage in financial planning: "Husbands, when you're trying to get your wife onboard, remember that she is wired for relationships and security. Asking her a question such as, 'How would it feel if we had ten thousand dollars in savings just for emergencies?' will get her attention." Ramsey then offers a second approach to punch her relational button: "Ninety-seven percent of women surveyed said they would like more communication in marriage. So what if you said, 'Honey, I was reading about how if we spent a few minutes a week working on a budget together, it would increase our communication in every area and ultimately create more intimacy and unity. Would you like to try that?' I'm willing to bet you won't need to say much more."[2]

After communicating your goals, the next step is to establish a budget designed to accomplish them. You should do this together or one of you could draft the budget for the two of you to go over to ensure agreement. The result should be a realistically achievable spending plan.

This initial budgeting should include a fund for emergencies. Murphy's Law always hovers, ready to smash your budget with an auto transmission going out or a home air conditioner blowing a compressor. If these emergencies pile up, or if they occur before your fund is large enough to cover them, you should agree up front on a plan B, which may include borrowing or drawing funds from regular savings.

You also need an up-front plan for windfall income, such as bequests, gifts, tax refunds, and so on. Without a plan such money usually gets blown away in the wind of the I've-scrimped-so-long-I-deserve-to-splurge syndrome. Agree in advance whether extra money will go to a fund within the budget, be shared discretionary money, or go to your church or a charity.

Your budget needs to include not only a plan for your

immediate income and outflow; it should also address long-range goals and needs. Crown Financial Ministries encourages spouses to discuss long-term financial goals: "This would include not only children's college educations, children's marriages, and retirement, but also what to do in the event that one spouse dies before the other."[3]

Budgeting means bookkeeping. Without managing and tracking your income and outflow, your budget will quickly get out of hand. One of you must be designated to manage your finances—paying the bills, updating the checkbook, maintaining records, and allocating funds according to the plan.

This must not be a financial takeover! Both should agree on which of you will manage the budget, and it should generally be the one who is best at math.

Though only one spouse manages the budget, both need to be savvy about everything in it. Both should know where the accounts and investments are located. And while I'm in the neighborhood, I'll throw in a bit of related advice at no extra charge: both of you must know the location of important papers such as insurance policies, property deeds, car titles, marriage license, wills, account numbers, the key to the lockbox, and so on.

BE MUTUALLY ACCOUNTABLE

Once a budget is agreed to, both you and your mate must determine to be dependable and trustworthy in sticking to it.

One step that will help is an ironclad pact that there will be no major purchases without mutual agreement between the two of you.

The potential difficulty in this rule is, of course, that the two of you will not always want the same things. When he wants a new fishing boat and she wants a new car, a calm and rational discussion is in order, or maybe a little attitude adjustment on the part of each. It's possible that both expenditures can be accommodated if they are made one at a time. Then the only item for discussion is who goes first.

Some financial advisers recommend that if the budget allows for discretionary spending—that is, if there is money left over after meeting all the necessary expenses and savings allocations—each spouse can have his and her own luxury spending fund within the account. While all other spending requires accountability, money in the spouse's own luxury fund does not. No matter how unnecessary one spouse may consider the other's purchase—her hundred-dollar fitness pants or his combination cell phone and razor—each can spend freely from his or her fund with no questions asked and no snide comments.

If you violate any principle of the budget, overspending in some area or making a major purchase the other didn't agree to, that money should be docked from your luxury spending fund.

SLAYING THE DRAGON OF DEBT

In today's consumer economy, we are continually urged to buy-buy-buy. You want a Lexus but you have a Chevy budget? No problem. Just sign this twenty-seven-page loan agreement promising lifetime indenture and your firstborn and you can park it in your garage today. You want a houseful of new furniture, jet skis, trail bikes, or a Caribbean cruise but you only have $28.19 in your savings account? No big deal. Just swipe one of your thirteen credit cards and it's yours right now.

Americans have been doing this for decades, and the result is an unprecedented nationwide load of personal debt amounting to 2.5 trillion dollars as of December 2011. The average household debt on credit cards alone is almost $16,000 per family.[4] Many of these households have several cards, all with outstanding balances, and making the minimum payments is one of their major monthly expenses.

I've heard financial advisers urge couples to cut up their credit cards. But in today's culture that is not always possible. You need credit cards for most online commerce, purchasing airline tickets, and renting cars. But one or two cards are enough. So make it a habit to shred all those credit card offers that clog your mailbox. To keep your card debt from getting out of hand, resolve to pay off the balance monthly, if possible, and leave only enough debt on the card to keep it active. Set a debt limit, and keep it low.

I realize that few couples can pay cash for everything they need, especially homes and cars. That's why we have mortgage companies and banks. Taking on a debt for a house—and usually for an automobile—is unavoidable for most couples. The common mistake, however, is in buying more house or car than your budget can sustain. When the monthly payments begin to loom, the budget can strain to the breaking point.

While most people see financing a car as unavoidable (and in many cases it is), the majority of car purchases are made long before they need to be. Glenn and Carrie's family sedan was six years old, and within the past year they had to replace the water pump, fix the alternator, and have the brake drums turned. Glenn figured it was time to trade, so he paid a visit to a local dealership.

It didn't take but a whiff of the new-car smell before he was drooling over a sparkling new SUV calling to him from the showroom. It had power everything, front and back air conditioning, a push-button sunroof, a built-in DVD player, and electric seat warmers. He got a pencil and gerrymandered the budget to accommodate the payments and presented the idea to Carrie.

She didn't warm to the purchase. She reminded Glenn of their teenage daughter's need for braces and all the costs involved with their son heading for college in the fall. Glenn was disappointed, but he didn't put up a fight because he knew she was right. When he actually compared the cost of the new car to maintaining the old one, he had to admit the purchase didn't make budgetary sense. New car payments for one year were quadruple the cost of last year's repairs on their present car. Being of sound mind, he realized his real problem was that driving his old car was not as cool or satisfying as driving a new one. He chucked his figures in the trash and actually let out a sigh of relief at not having to face the strain of an over-extended budget.

To avoid financial disaster, you must close your ears to the siren voices of government and alluring TV commercials urging you to spend your way to prosperity.

Even when it does come time for Glenn to trade, buying a fairly recent model, vetted used car is much more economically efficient than absorbing the enormous depreciation that occurs the moment you drive a new one off the lot. And he can get that new-car smell with a little aroma tablet from his local carwash.

To avoid financial disaster, you must close your ears to the siren voices of government and alluring TV commercials urging you to spend your way to prosperity and swipe your card at every store in town. Lead yourself not into temptation. If you love watching the specials on the Home Shopping or QVC networks, reprogram your remote to skip those channels.

Many people love to go shopping even if they have no need to buy anything. The daughter of a friend of mine shops so much that someone gave her a large pin-on button reading, "I shop, therefore I am." Going shopping almost always results in a purchase, and it's a subtle snare that can quickly cause debt to soar. If you love to shop, know your spending limit and stick to it.

If you are already deeply in debt, stop all discretionary spending and devote those funds to paying off your debt. If you cannot adjust your budget to do this, then contact one of the many services that offer help and budgetary advice for families with unmanageable debt.

FORCE YOURSELVES TO SAVE

As a result of our national buying binge, per capita savings are at their lowest point in America's history. This means many families with two wage earners and above-average incomes are living paycheck to paycheck, struggling with debt, and failing to save. They are highly vulnerable to financial disaster because they have no financial cushion to break their fall.

Saving is a necessary factor in responsible budgeting. Saving enables you to handle emergencies that would otherwise blow your budget to smithereens. Saving prepares you for retirement when your income will be lower or nonexistent. It enables you to make large purchases without going into debt.

And it enables you to accumulate funds for your children's education.

There are many ways to save. Among these are IRAs, 401(k)s, CDs, US Treasury notes, and savings accounts. I recommend that you consult a financial adviser to determine which is best for you. Remember that investments are not savings. Investments should be considered risks to be made only out of discretionary funds. Never invest more than you can afford to lose.

If you don't save because you lack the discipline, own up to it and find a solution. One solution is automatic payroll deduction by your employer to a program such as a 401(k) account. Another is to automatically split your paycheck deposit, putting a preplanned percentage into savings before you ever touch any of the money. Using these methods, your savings, like your tax deduction, comes out of money you never see and thus you don't miss it.

The golden rule that enables saving is always to spend less than you earn. That is the real way to build financial security. Most people today tend to spend just a little more than they earn, which means their budget is always expanding like hot air in a balloon and putting increasing pressure on their income. If your income is low, that simply means your lifestyle choices need to be scaled to fit what you make. Your dream house, luxury car, and updated entertainment center may have to wait, but your savings should continue. The reason most people fail to save is that they have been conditioned to mistake extras for necessities.

One good way to balance responsible spending and saving is to buy wisely. Compare prices, look for sales. Thrift stores and consignment shops often have good bargains on clothing or furniture that appear to be new. Carolyn MacInnes offers a great list of practical money-saving tips on the Focus on the Family website.[5]

WHOSE MONEY IS IT, ANYWAY?

As you work with your family finances, it is imperative that you remember whose money you're dealing with. As Christians, we understand that everything in this universe belongs to God, and that includes your money. Christ made this principle clear in the parable of the bags of gold in Matthew 25. As you remember, a businessman gave three servants a certain number of bags of gold to care for individually while he went away on a journey. When he returned, he required each servant to account for how he had used the money entrusted to him.

It's the same with us. God entrusts to each of us however much money he thinks we can handle, and he will demand an accounting as to whether we used it well or poorly. This does not necessarily mean just your tithe; it covers the whole gamut of how you handle money. Do you squander it on yourself or blow it on meaningless frivolities? Or do you use it to help others or to foster solid values in your life and that of your family?

Financial responsibility before God includes tithing. Throughout biblical history tithing has been required of God's people. Abraham tithed to the priest-king Melchizedek (Genesis 14:18–20). God commanded Israel to tithe (Leviticus 27:30). The prophet Malachi told Israel that by withholding their tithes, they were robbing God, which would result in disaster (3:8–9). On the other hand, he promised overflowing blessings if they tithed: "'Test me in this,' says the LORD Almighty, 'and see if I will not throw open the floodgates of heaven and pour out so much blessing that there will not be room enough to store it'" (v. 10 NIV).

We know this promise is for us as well, for Christ himself affirmed the principle: "Give, and it will be given to you. A good measure, pressed down, shaken together and running over, will be poured into your lap. For with the measure you use, it will be measured to you" (Luke 6:38 NIV).

We are told to tithe not because God needs the money. He owns the universe! It's because we need to give. Giving shows our dedication to God and curbs our natural tendency toward selfishness. It also reminds us of our total dependence on God for everything we have and gives us a way to acknowledge it and show our gratitude. The resulting rewards he promises are merely his way of expressing his approval for our being responsible.

With prayer and planning, you and your spouse can be on the same page financially.

With prayer and planning, you and your spouse can be on the same page financially. You can have unified clarity concerning your use of money. You can give up self-reliance or irresponsible presumption upon God and be set free—financially free. What a way to live!

THINGS TO DO
TO ENSURE YOU AND YOUR SPOUSE
SPEND MONEY RESPONSIBLY

———⟨O⟩———

- Talk frankly and deeply about the experience and expectations about money each of you bring into the marriage.

- Be honest about your money situation, what you owe, how much you make, how much discretionary income you have.

- Develop a budget together and both of you address individual needs, wants and expectations so you are both on board.

- Request the two of you attend a financial seminar that might bring new insights to your spouse.

- Spend time talking to your spouse about your dreams, hopes, and desires of what life would be like in twenty years. Paint a picture of what a financially free future looks like and show how much money will be needed to get to that future.

- Evaluate your approach to finances to ensure you are not motivated by a need to control versus a desire for future financial freedom.

- Request that the two of you talk to a financial counselor or adviser from a ministry like Crown Financial Ministries.
- Celebrate every debt paid off and every other positive consequence of your responsible choices.

6

Practice Lifetime Vows

To watch a short video on this subject, go to
7MinuteMarriageSolution.com/13

What do you do when your spouse is unfaithful? Do you stay or do you go? Just a few days ago I was talking to a man whose wife had broken their wedding vows. Most men don't keep their wedding vows after the wife has broken hers, but this exceptional man did. He realized he was not a perfect husband, and he wondered whether he might have done things that contributed to her unfaithfulness. He chose not to divorce her as long as the two of them got help for their problems.

But after he made that decision, the plot thickened. A test revealed that she was pregnant by another man. But this man of character still did not waver in his commitment. He had made a vow to love her when they married, and he was determined to do what he said he would do. When the baby was born he adopted her and loved her as his own. He made her a vow that he would be her father no matter what. Now that was a man who understood what it means to keep a vow!

Today we tend to use the word *promise* more than *vow*, but they are the same thing: a binding commitment to do what you say you will do. When a person makes a vow, he gives his word, and when he gives his word, his integrity is on the line. A person's word is closely identified with the person himself. His word reveals his character and tells us who he is. The apostle John asserts this fact most dramatically in the first words of his gospel where he identifies Jesus as the Word of God—the emanation or expression of God that reveals God's character.

This binding connection between a person and his word is why God looks upon a vow as an extremely serious thing. As Moses writes, "When a man makes a vow to the Lord or takes an oath to obligate himself by a pledge, he must not break his word but must do everything he said" (Numbers 30:2 NIV).

God looks upon a vow as an extremely serious thing.

Obviously the people of the Bible understood the high seriousness of a vow and acted accordingly. Today we have largely lost that awareness. I presume that most people who make promises intend to keep them. But if keeping a promise becomes inconvenient or difficult, all too many feel justified in breaking it.

As we all know, politicians provide the model for promise-breaking. Vows to them seem to be like your mother's pie crusts: easily made, easily broken. Most pundits believe that President George H. W. Bush lost his bid for reelection because he reneged on a particularly important campaign promise. During the 1988 campaign he famously promised, "Read my lips: no new taxes." When he subsequently agreed to raise taxes, the broken promise became his downfall in the 1992 election.

I suspect that today married couples have overtaken politicians as the worst vow-breakers. Nowhere is today's lax attitude toward vows more evident than in marriages. Couples stand before a minister clasping each other's hands and vow to love each other "in sickness and in health, for better or for worse, till death do us part." It is a solemn promise, a lifetime commitment before God and witnesses that they will remain faithful and true to each other throughout their lives. But any inconvenience, any conflict, any problem, any loss of attractiveness or romantic feeling, or any appealing man or woman on the other side of the fence often causes either partner to renege on the vow and break up the marriage.

FOUR CAUSES OF BROKEN WEDDING VOWS

There may be a thousand excuses for breaking wedding vows, but God condones only two as valid reasons: abandonment and adultery. In cases of unfaithfulness, the offended party is justified in leaving the marriage because the other person broke the vow (Matthew 19:8–9). This frees the innocent party from adhering to it.

The only other justifiable divorce situation detailed in Scripture is when a spouse who is an unbeliever abandons the believing spouse (1 Corinthians 7:14–15). These are the exceptions where divorce can be initiated on biblical grounds. In every other situation the believer is admonished to seek a solution to the problem rather than to divorce.

Aside from unfaithfulness, however, I believe about 99.9 percent of broken marriage vows stem in some way from sheer selfishness. The marriage turns out not to be what you wanted. It's harder than you expected, not as exciting; it cramps your style, it ties you down, it requires too much give and take, your mate has flaws you didn't expect, or you don't get along very well.

Over the years I have found that most of this selfishness falls under one or more of the following four categories—routine, regret, rule-breaking, or risky choices. Let's explore these categories one by one.

ROUTINE

Like in the old Johnny Cash/June Carter song "Jackson," Eddie and Kristi were quite feverish and joined together in holy matrimony in an emotional state that exceeded the degree of heat from the most intense and potent pepper sauce. But now the honeymoon is long over. The heat has cooled; the urgency of compelling sexual need has been worked out of their system. Over time a repeated pattern has developed: Both go to work every day and come home tired. They eat out or cook something easy, then he loads the dishwasher while she rounds up the dirty clothes and stuffs them in the washing machine. She helps the kids with their homework while he does the work he brought home from the office. After the ten o'clock news, they shower, peck each other on the cheek, and plop into bed. The next day is a rerun of the same, as is the day after.

Both Eddie and Kristi feel that their life is slipping away. Their appeal will soon fade, and they wonder if there is more to life than they are experiencing. It's a sure setup for a midlife crisis.

So when a good-looking marketing director at a trade convention asks Kristi to dine with him several times and finally suggests further intimacies, she begins to feel that she has missed out on what she really wanted in marriage. This may be her last chance at happiness. Suddenly her vow to Eddie seems a small, distant thing. Surely she has a right to happiness. After all, that's what life is about, isn't it?

REGRET

Now let's look at Eddie. The dullness of his marriage (as he perceives it) leads him to daydream about his high school sweetheart, Megan, the girl he almost married. He remembers how beautiful she was, especially on those moonlit nights in his parked car overlooking the town. He wonders whatever happened to her and decides to look her up on Facebook. *Ah, there she is. Wow! She's still gorgeous!* He invites her to be a Facebook friend. They exchange a number of messages, and he finds out that she is married but unhappy. *Why didn't I marry her when I had the chance?* He begins to regret not marrying Megan, and suddenly his vow to Kristi looms like a boulder blocking his path to real happiness.

Eddie doesn't realize that he has created an illusion. He thinks he is grieving the loss of the woman he didn't marry who could have made him much happier than the one he did. He does not realize that he is idealizing Megan into something she is not and never was. Memory tends to edit the past, elevating the romantic, happy times and submerging the conflicts and the uncertainties. He can't see that if he had married Megan, he would have encountered the same problems as with Kristi, or maybe worse. He regrets not having what he thinks he really wanted, which prevents him from accepting, appreciating, and loving the woman he has.

RISKY CHOICES

When Kristi chose to accept the invitations to dine with the handsome marketing director, she was making a risky choice.

She was entering a high danger zone where one false step could cause her to slip and fall. Even worse, she was entering that zone with someone eager to trip her deliberately.

When Eddie connected to his old high school sweetheart on Facebook, he too made a risky choice. It was the perfect setup for an online affair, which often leads to physical affairs. According to a 2009 Loyola University study, "Facebook is cited in one out of every five divorces in the United States."[1]

Suppose Eddie's old sweetheart urges him to attend their high school reunion and meet her face-to-face. Before he responds, he had better think through what might happen in the future if he accepts. In this prerecording of his potential future, he meets Megan and she is bubbly and excited to see him, just as when they were dating. They dance, and she moves closer to him and softens in his arms. He returns home with her much on his mind, and they exchange e-mails and then a few clandestine calls. On a business trip he detours to the town where she lives. They have dinner, and one thing leads to another until she is in his hotel room that night.

The tape of the future continues: After the affair Eddie is even unhappier with his marriage, and he divorces Kristi and marries Megan. The prerecording continues along predictable lines, showing what will happen on down the line. He is marrying a cheater. When the glow wears off their marriage, won't she do it again? Won't he?

It doesn't take an Einstein to know that some situations are risky and should be avoided. That doesn't mean avoiding them later after things start getting out of hand; it means avoiding that first step into the risk zone.

Jim was happily married. At the end of a stressful workday his beautiful young administrative assistant asked him to give her a shoulder rub. Jim did, and as he kneaded her shoulders, she kept moaning, "Oh, that feels soooo good! You really know how to use your hands." The next time it was her shoulders and neck. The next time it was . . . well, you know where things went from there. But the truth is, things were headed there from the beginning.

Frank had successfully resisted porn. But once when his wife was out of town, a salacious e-mail ad popped up on his computer. Curious, he clicked on the icon, which led him to a porn site. He couldn't resist the nude images enticing him there, and he entered the site. From that moment on, he was hooked, and he returned again and again.

Jim and Frank made risky choices and they paid the price. Eddie and Kristi face similar choices. All too often those choices, once made, lead one deeper and deeper into a maelstrom from which people find it almost impossible to extract themselves. Marriage vows are broken, either overtly by seeking divorce or more subtly by violating the promise to love and honor your mate to the exclusion of all others. The only sure way to prevent the downward pull is to resist taking that first, risky step. Once you take it, the other steps become increasingly harder to resist. As Mark Twain said, "It's easier to stay out than get out."

Refusing to plunge into those risky choices before they get a grip on you is a big step toward remaining faithful in your marriage. Every time I refuse to ogle another woman or lust after her I am practicing my vows. Each time I turn the page to avoid a magazine ad featuring a scantily clad model, I am practicing my vows. Every time I honor my wife in a conversation with a friend rather than put her in a negative light, I am practicing my vows. And every time I refuse to click on a website or view a scene in a movie or steer my focus toward another female, I am practicing my vows as an act of commitment to her.

Every time my wife resists the temptation to compare me to another man she is practicing her vows to me. Every time she refuses to read an erotic novel or some unrealistic romance tale, she is practicing her vows to me. Every time she refuses to connect online with someone she dated, she is practicing her vows to me. And every time she refuses to fantasize about someone she sees in a movie or on television, she is practicing her vows to me. In practicing vows in these initial ways, we avoid breaking them in horrific ways.

When a mate does not practice visual, emotional, and social fidelity, the end result is often sexual infidelity.

RULE-BREAKING

Marriage psychologist Dr. Willard F. Harley lists four basic rules designed to help couples fulfill their marriage vows. These rules, which we will explore more fully in a moment, include commitments to each other in the areas of care, protection, honesty, and time.[2]

When Eddie and Kristi stood at the altar and repeated their wedding vows, rules didn't even enter their minds. They gladly made those vows because they were so madly in love that remaining faithful and true was going to be a slam dunk. But a few years into the marriage, the need for those vows became apparent. That hidden, ugly foot appeared. Reality settled in, unsuspected traits emerged, disagreements arose, and the drone of humdrum routine dulled their romance. They found that they didn't always feel like doing the right thing. They felt the urge to do what they wanted instead of what they ought— the urge to follow their feelings rather than to exercise self-discipline and selfless giving.

If we always felt like doing the right thing,
we wouldn't need laws.

That's why we have laws and rules. They prod us to do the right thing even when we don't feel like it. If we always felt like doing the right thing, we wouldn't need laws. Wedding vows are crucial because in the presence of witnesses the couple makes a solemn promise to stick to the rules even when they feel the powerful pull of their wants and urges. Rules remind us to do what love should make us want to do.

THE ROMANCE OF THE RULES

In order to start practicing their lifetime vows, Eddie and Kristi need to do two things. First, they need to spark up and rejuvenate their marriage. When you read that sentence, you probably start thinking of things like more dates, more surprises, more romance, more variety in sex. These changes are all worth considering, but it may surprise you to know that you can spark up your marriage simply by following Dr. Harley's four rules previously mentioned—care, protection, honesty, and time.

CARE

Commit to the rule of care and you commit to meeting each other's needs—emotionally, sexually, spiritually, and physically. It means expressing your love and showing your affection. This includes touches, kisses, hugs, cards, courtesies, and gifts. Care means being the other's companion, both in building a life together and in recreational activities. It means being your mate's conversational companion, building intimacy by communicating freely with each other. It may be the most difficult thing you do, but sitting and listening is the communication vehicle of caring. Words still need to be expressed, but sometimes a listening ear is the strongest expression of care.

PROTECTION

Primarily, I view the rule of protection as a function the husband provides for his wife. That means providing a secure home and a safe environment for her and the family. It means accompanying your wife in dangerous areas and defending her against threats of harm. But there are many ways in which both husbands and wives should protect each other. They should protect each other's time, reputation, health, shared secrets, and privacy.

HONESTY

The rule of honesty means being open and transparent with each other. It means holding nothing back, expressing your true feelings, longings, hopes, failures, and needs. The way to intimacy is opening up your hearts to each other and giving your mate full access to who you are.

TIME

The rule of time is something that both partners must honor. Time must be planned, not stumbled upon. Time must be a priority, not a luxury. It needs to include time for eyeball-to-eyeball contact. It needs to include listening and sharing and resolving. It must be consistent and dedicated solely to each other. Young children, needy parents, fantastic friends, or an amazing hobby must never be allowed to eliminate your time together. [3]

Now you can see what I mean when I say that following rules can rejuvenate your marriage. Built into these rules are the very rejuvenating factors every marriage thrives on. While the idea of following rules doesn't seem very loving or romantic, the truth is that the rules keep love and romance rolling by putting us on the track when our lethargy or wandering feelings lure us to go astray. Following these rules makes your wedding vows much easier to keep.

FROM A PARTY TO A PROJECT

The second thing that would help Eddie and Kristi commit to keeping their vows is to change their view of what marriage is really about. If they can do this, they will find that their marriage is not quite as bad as they think it is. Part of their problem is that, like so many couples, they plunged into marriage thinking it would be a party instead of a project. If it's a party, you expect nothing but good times, fun, and frolic. But if it's a project, that means it involves discipline, work, and goals to be achieved.

I can guess what you're thinking now: making marriage a project takes out all the joy and turns it into a chore. Not so.

In fact, the opposite is true. When you think of marriage as a party and then things start going wrong—an argument breaks out, someone gets sick, a storm comes and everyone has to get out of the pool—the party is ruined. It's over and you have nothing to show for it but the mess to be cleaned up.

But when you think of marriage as a project, when difficulties arise you take them in stride. You know that every worthwhile endeavor has its snags. You work through them, and joy comes when the problem is solved and you move on to the next step. Almost all projects involve times of dull routine. A Carnegie Hall concert by a great pianist requires hours and hours of repetitive practice. It's dull, it's tiring, but the end result is breathtaking, spine-tingling music. The everyday things you do in marriage may seem dull and repetitive, but they are building a life together—an achievement that will give you great joy and satisfaction.

Projects can be exhilarating, but not everything involved in them is fun. For me, writing this book is a project. I began it with excitement and great hopes. As I got into it, there were times when I bogged down or got stuck on what I should write next or how to say it in the best way. At times I deleted what I had written and started over. But in plowing through these obstacles, I find gratification in each completed paragraph, each chapter. The momentary obstacles and the tedious hours of research don't put me off because I'm focused on the goal of getting the book into the hands of people it can help.

That's the kind of change in outlook Eddie and Kristi need. It's not so much a change in the substance of their marriage—the work and routine of keeping things running—but rather a change in attitude toward what they are doing.

What Eddie and Kristi now see as a dull and monotonous trap can be seen as a thing of beauty. A stronger focus on the harmony of the music they are performing together can cause the tedium of doing scales to be caught up in the joy of mutual accomplishment. Such a change can cause them to see their vows as they did when they married—so motivated by love for each other that living up to them will be a slam dunk. Expect nothing but a party, and you get nothing but a mess to clean up. Expect to tackle a glorious project, and great joy and satisfaction will come as an unexpected by-product.

THE UNHAPPY CONSEQUENCE
OF BROKEN VOWS

Breaking wedding vows never leads to anything good. It's either a broken marriage with all the legal, emotional, financial, spiritual, and family fallout that follows, or it's the grueling ordeal of confession, repentance, forgiveness, and rebuilding the shattered relationship from the ground up.

The happiness you expect to find in breaking out of a dull marriage and marrying the partner of your dreams is a myth. People who break vows are not happier. According to the Institute for American Values, "Two-thirds of unhappily married spouses who stayed married reported that their marriages were happy five years later." Or, to flip the coin, "Unhappily married adults who divorced were no happier than unhappily married adults who stayed married. . . . Even unhappy spouses who had divorced and remarried were no happier on average than those who stayed married."[4]

The happiness you expect to find in
breaking out of a dull marriage and marrying
the partner of your dreams is a myth.

Breaking your wedding vow reveals the truth about your character. It says you are not a person of integrity; your word cannot be trusted. Without a strong commitment to personal integrity, you cannot be happy with yourself, and if you are unhappy with yourself, you cannot be happy with your spouse. While you don't realize it, your unhappiness is not coming from your mate; it's coming from inside yourself.

The absence of character revealed by broken vows explains why they are likely to be broken again. It only makes sense that second marriages end at the rate of 60 to 67 percent and third marriages at a whopping 70 to 73 percent.[5] What else should you expect from a person who does not honor a vow? Marry a person who cheats on his or her spouse, and you can expect to be cheated on.

Of course you don't expect that to happen in your second marriage. You believe you are the exception. You believe you are so amazing that this person who cheated with you would never cheat on you. Most likely you will discover how wrong you can be.

The Bible is very clear that there are exceptions to the rule of no divorce. If your spouse has abandoned you or committed adultery, you have permission from Jesus to divorce. But even when your marriage hits a major pothole like adultery, abuse, or addiction, it is not imperative that you break it off. You can take either of two distinct directions. One, of course, is to divorce. This is the way most accepted by today's culture. But over and over I find that couples who stay together and work through the issues that led to the infidelity build marriages that are often much stronger than those that have not faced such a major challenge. Though awfully painful, the process builds character, which every happy person must have whether married or not. We all need to start realizing that character is vitally important—even more important than our immediate wants, as did the man in the following true story.

General George C. Marshall, US Army chief of staff during World War II and later secretary of defense and secretary of state, married Elizabeth (Lily) Cole in 1902 when he was a twenty-one-year-old second lieutenant. On their wedding night, she revealed that because of a medical condition she could never have sex. George Marshall's new wife knew and chose not to reveal it until they were married. Most young men would have felt enormously betrayed by such a revelation, no doubt ending the marriage immediately. But not George Marshall. He had made a vow, and he felt duty bound not only to remain married—but also to fulfill his vow by treating his wife with love and honor.

Throughout their twenty-five-year marriage (she died in 1927), he was never unfaithful to her. According to biographer Ed Cray, "Marshall lavished a hundred little attentions on Lily. . . . He fetched and carried. He planned little surprises. He was solicitous about her health and comfort. . . . He paid her innumerable little compliments. . . . He gave her his unremitting consideration, smoothed the path before his queen and led her by his hand."[6]

This kind of character and integrity seems extraordinary and even beyond comprehension today. But it should be the norm for everyone. To be a person of integrity before God, you must practice your lifetime vows. You do it because you said you would. It may not be easy, but I can assure you that it's the ultimate way to joy.

THINGS TO DO
TO PRACTICE LIFETIME VOWS
— ⟨⟩ —

- Start to view your vow of faithfulness as all encompassing rather than a mere promise of sexual fidelity.
- Keeping vows requires character so build yours if you struggle.
- Intimate connection eliminates most of the power of temptation so invest in deeper connection.
- "I'm not hurting anyone " is the common lie the unfaithful tell themselves.
- The standard for faithfulness is known by, approved by and involving your spouse.
- Keeping your vows to God results in keeping your vows to your spouse (or faithfulness to God secures faithfulness to your spouse).
- The best way to start keeping your vows is to marry someone you know you can build a lifetime of trust together so be smart before you start down the aisle.
- Avoiding temptation results in not succumbing to it.

7

Show Respect No Matter What

To watch a short video on this subject, go to
7MinuteMarriageSolution.com/14

One of the most surprising realities I see in marriage today is how frequently spouses endure appalling disrespect from each other. It is not an exaggeration to say that mates often show more respect to strangers than to each other. Many husbands and wives discount each other, they are dismissive, or they openly ridicule each other in public. They go far beyond a mere lack of acceptance to finding ways to overtly put down each other or simply ignore the other. Outside of infidelity, disrespect is the most destructive behavior in any marriage.

This is so prevalent and so devastating that repeatedly respect comes up as the most important thing that needs to be there as a foundation for every marriage. Both men and women in the survey I did cited it as the number-one most important thing. Just about every problem can be boiled down to a lack of respect. Adultery is the ultimate lack of respect for your spouse, the institution of marriage, and for God. You can't respect a person while criticizing, trying to change, nagging, hiding money from, or ignoring your spouse.

When there is strong mutual respect, it supports all the other areas needed for a marriage to grow. If respect is not there, that does not mean your marriage is hopeless. You can find respect and give it to your spouse even after years of disrespectful treatment. Let's start with an example of a guy who understood how to show respect to his wife.

When Stan and Lindsey bought their new SUV, they didn't reckon on it being almost too large for their garage. The new vehicle had to be eased in and backed out with great care. Stan hung a tennis ball from the ceiling that touched the center of the windshield exactly when the vehicle should be stopped. "There's almost no wiggle room front-to-back or side-to-side," he told Lindsey. "That means we must always back out with great care to keep from causing damage."

For two months all went well. But one morning Lindsey overslept, putting an important doctor appointment in jeopardy. In her haste, she thrust the gearshift into reverse and hit the gas pedal. As the car zipped out of the garage she heard a sickening crunch as the right side mirror caught the edge of the door frame and buckled like a bulldozed tree.

Stan and Lindsey had recently joined a small Bible study group, and on Sunday night they were hosting the event in their home for the first time. As the couples sat around chatting, one of the men said, "Stan, at church I noticed the crunched mirror on your new SUV. What happened?"

Lindsey held her breath. She was about to be embarrassed and humiliated in front of her new friends.

"Well," Stan responded, "I guess you could say that both Lindsey and I messed up that mirror. One night when I pulled into the garage after working late, I parked the car a tad too far to the right. I should have backed out and reparked, but I was too tired to bother. So the next morning when Lindsey backed out, naturally the mirror caught on the garage door frame."

Lindsey relaxed. It was all she could do to keep from kissing that wonderful man of hers right there in front of everyone.

Stan's response showed his great respect for his wife. He could have done what many husbands do in similar situations. He could have humiliated her with a dumb blonde joke or a deprecating comment about women drivers. Or he could honestly have pointed out that she had ignored his precautions. But he considered his wife's feelings and spared her the humiliation. That is respect.

Respect is the number-one attribute that couples want more of in their marriage. Nothing contributes more toward feeling love or being loved than respect. It is the mother stream from which rivers of blessings will flow into all areas of a marriage.

Build respect and you build your relationship. Destroy respect and you negate most of the other positive attributes you bring into the relationship. I think a great place to start in evaluating your role in the relationship is to ask this simple question: "How much do I respect my spouse?" Then ask the follow-up question: "How often and how deeply do I show it?"

Respect grows out of seeing your mate as a person—a marvel of creation highly valued in God's eyes, yet one who is flawed and struggling with sin and selfishness just as you are. When you learn to see your mate as a marvelous gift of God, you will see him or her as the most precious being in your life, to be valued and cherished above all others. We naturally respect and treat well the things we value. But somehow when it comes to one's spouse, that treatment often deteriorates. We revert to our natural self-centeredness and let our moods, irritations, disappointments, or self-interest dictate our behavior. We fail to demonstrate the love we should have for our mates, and that adds up to disrespect.

DISRESPECT: A MAJOR WALL-BUILDER

Disrespect, whether in large things or small, comes in many forms—putdowns, rudeness, failure to praise, ignoring, thoughtlessness, and lack of trust, to name a few. The underlying cause of disrespect that lies beneath these behaviors is *objectification*. When you objectify a person, you see him or her as a thing—something to be used for your benefit. Objectifying people means they can be ignored, mistreated, or swept aside when they are not meeting a need. Husbands objectify wives by using them as objects rather than valuing them as humans. She becomes his means of sexual pleasure, of getting children, or of having his meals prepared. Wives objectify husbands by valuing them primarily as a source of income, a meal ticket, or a means of security or having a family.

In my opening example, Stan had a perfect opportunity to objectify his wife by using her as an object of put-down humor. In my experience, Stan's choice to refrain from embarrassing her is not typical. I hear put-downs of mates at nearly every social gathering I attend: "Harry just can't fix anything. Last week it took him two hours and three trips to Home Depot to repair a little faucet leak. And he ended up calling a plumber anyway." "Melinda messes up every joke she tells—always puts the punch line from one joke at the end of another." "I try to get Phil to exercise, but he just lolls in his La-Z-Boy every night and stares at the TV." "Renee tried to make a casserole last week. None of us could eat it, so I gave to the dog. He wouldn't eat it either." "Yes, we'd love to take a cruise, but with what Bob earns it looks like we'll have to settle for another vacation at his mom's."

A husband or wife who makes such comments may think it's merely a harmless form of the common banter that makes up the ongoing battle of the sexes. But this banter is not harmless; it can leave casualties. Maybe the comment is meant for humor, but the element of put-down is there. While the partner may choose to let it roll off, there's usually enough "dig" involved to cause some degree of inner pain. The willingness of a spouse to tease or belittle the other, either in public or private, is a passive-aggressive way of objectifying and discounting your spouse, and it is an obvious symptom of disrespect.

I use a lot of stories and humor in my speaking. I can assure you that if I tell a story about my wife, I have already cleared it with her. And afterward you can be sure we will talk about whether the story accomplished what was intended and how it made her feel. If I don't take those precautions, it is only a matter of time before we will be discussing why we feel distant from each other. The last thing I want to do is make her feel uncomfortable or look bad in the eyes of others. To that end she is never made the butt of my jokes. You cannot treat a spouse that way and expect her to be drawn to you.

One of the most common signs of disrespect is simple rudeness, or a lack of common courtesy. After a long day at the office soothing his boss and coddling clients, at home the husband thinks he should be able to relax and "be himself." Often this means he feels justified in dropping all effort to be kind or mannerly. He plops down in his recliner and flips on the news, brushing away his children as they tug at him for attention. His wife brings him a glass of tea and says cheerily, "How was work today?"

"How can you think I'd want to talk about work right now?" he snarls. "Can't you get these screaming brats out of here so I can have a little peace and quiet before dinner?"

The man is thinking only of himself and failing to value his wife, who is doing nothing more than showing interest in him. Scenes like this occur daily all over the nation. It is nothing short of simple disrespect, and it pushes couples apart.

Often people are more respectful toward strangers and people they work with than to the most important person in their life.

I urge you to take the time to evaluate on a regular basis the way you speak to your husband or wife. Often people are more respectful toward strangers and people they work with than to the most important person in their life. They put on their best face when dealing with others, but they tear down and shatter the person who will be there in their future. The more you build up a spouse, the brighter that future is going to be.

Another way spouses disrespect each other is through thoughtlessness. This shows itself in several ways, among them the common complaint that "He never remembers my birthday or our anniversary." Thoughtlessness also occurs when couples fail to pay compliments. He fails to notice her new dress or the new style of her hair. She fails to compliment him on losing twenty pounds. Kind attentiveness needs to become a style of communicating in every marriage, but it is almost impossible if you are holding a grudge or feeding a justifiable resentment. This is where counseling can greatly benefit the two of you. It assists you in wiping the slate clean so that compliments can flow freely and sincerely from your heart.

Disrespect shows up in our failure to express appreciation. She wanted a space to set up an easel and paint. So he spent many evenings and Saturdays designing and building an additional room onto the house. When he finished, it never occurred to her to offer even a simple "thank you." To reward him with a romantic weekend for just the two of them would have been even better.

Disrespect occurs when husbands and wives fail to show interest in the other's achievements. When the kids left home she took up quilting. She did beautiful work, and when she showed him a completed quilt on which she had spent over a hundred hours, he glanced up momentarily from the TV and muttered, "That's nice, dear."

When he retired he bought a rusted '57 Chevy and spent months restoring it to pristine condition. When he proudly showed his wife the finished product, her only comment was, "You don't plan on keeping that old car in our garage, do you?"

It's a sign of disrespect when couples take for granted the everyday work the other does. She cooks, does laundry, cares for the kids, and cleans the house. If he ever thinks about any of these chores, he takes them for granted as just what wives do. He never expresses appreciation. And it works the other way as well. He works eight hours, fights traffic, keeps the yard mowed and trimmed, makes house and plumbing repairs, and helps clean the dinner dishes. In her mind, that's merely what husbands are supposed to do, so it never occurs to her to thank him for it.

A serious evidence of disrespect is breaching the other's trust. When Marty reached his late forties, he began to experience sexual dysfunction. Frustrated and embarrassed, he promised his wife he would see a physician and implored her not to tell a soul about what he was going through. Fortunately the problem was a hormonal imbalance easily solved. But a week or so later a golfing buddy said he'd heard that Marty was having a "little problem" and offered the name of a doctor.

Mortified, Marty confronted his wife, who confessed that she had told only her closest friend, who promised not to breathe a word to anyone.

Marty realized that word of his very private problem had undoubtedly reached many ears, and his humiliation was deep enough that he considered quitting his job and moving to a distant town. Sharing confidences that should be tightly kept between a husband and wife is a serious example of disrespect.

Any lack of attention or failure to consider the other's feelings is a form of disrespect. It can show up in many other ways that can easily go unnoticed by the one committing the offense. Among these are shaming, blaming, ignoring, provoking, patronizing, dismissing, and controlling. These failures may seem small and inconsequential, but they deprive marriages of the oil that keeps the wheels turning smoothly. Without mutual respect, couples drift apart, and eventually the marriage can grind to a halt.

Any lack of attention or failure to consider
the other's feelings is a form of disrespect.

In my own desire to show more and more respect to my wife, I did some soul searching and came up with something I had not considered before. I am very time conscious and rarely late to any event or appointment. My wife is not that conscious of time. She is conscious of people—making connections and building relationships. I found myself frequently wanting to move her along to the next thing. Most of the time, the next thing could wait or was not much of a priority. I realized I was using my desire to manage her time as a way to control. I did not see this until I looked below the surface and saw that I really wanted her to abide by my timetable. Essentially I wanted her to show respect to me by complying with my rush. But in so doing I was disrespecting her and the parts of her personality that I still marvel at. Today, respecting her in this area has produced a lot less stress for me as I have turned over *my* agenda and submitted to *our* agenda out of respect for her.

WHY WE MUST RESPECT EACH OTHER

In his famous discourse "The Weight of Glory" C. S. Lewis points out that humans are not "mere mortals." Men and women are not ordinary creatures; we are eternal beings created in the image of God (Genesis 1:27) and worthy of respect.[1] Though God's image in us has been dimmed and blurred by the fall, it is still there beneath our crust of sin, and we bear the capacity to become creatures of dazzling beauty and glory. So both our origin and our destiny give us a strong basis for respecting each other.

Nowhere should that respect be greater or more diligently expressed than in marriage, where two complementary reflectors of the divine image are bonded in a unique love relationship ordained by God himself. Each partner in a marriage must treat the other as a precious being, dearly loved by God. Your mate is paying you the high compliment of lifetime commitment, and that deserves your deepest love, honor, and respect.

CEMENT YOUR MARRIAGE WITH RESPECT

If you have problems with any of the disrespectful behaviors I've addressed above, it's no good trying to justify your failures with excuses such as, "That's just the way I am" or "I just don't have the time" or "She understands how I am" or "He's just too sensitive about little things." If, for example, you have slipped into a habit of being critical of your husband or wife, that habit can be broken. And breaking it will do much to bring the two of you closer.

If you habitually forget birthdays, anniversaries, and special days such as Valentine's or Mother's Day, you can take decisive steps to change that habit. Get a calendar. Put reminders in your computer, tablet, or phone. You keep business and dental appointments made weeks or months in advance; so you can certainly work into your schedule a way to remember your mate on special occasions. And remember them in ways they appreciate most. Don't send flowers to a woman who would rather you show respect for how hard she works by cleaning the entire house before she awakes on your anniversary.

You can also show your respect by speaking well of her at all times. Do it in front of people around you in person. Do it on social media too. What a great thing to see something respectful and loving for all the world to see! I remember when Misty posted that she loved being married to me. That was amazing to me. Anyone and everyone can say I love my spouse. But to say you love being married to your spouse takes it to a deeper, more meaningful level. At least it did for me.

Maybe you're not a good handyman. You're all thumbs when working with household tools. Still, when you married you took on the responsibility of keeping the house repaired and its plumbing and appliances working. The house is highly important to a wife. It's the nesting place for her family, and to have it snug, neat, and in working order is a big factor in her sense of security. She may subliminally interpret your failure to attend to broken appliances, leaky roofs, peeling paint, and loose carpet as a lack of love, and certainly as a lack of respect. That doesn't mean you must do all these things yourself, but it's important to be attentive to them—spot the problem quickly and either fix it yourself or promptly call a serviceman. Many repairs are easier for klutzes to make now than in the past, as manufacturers have simplified parts and assembly.

I once read a statement by some male celebrity whose name I've forgotten. He said, "It is impossible for a man to treat a woman too well." I think he's right on the money. The simplest way of treating a woman well is to show respect through common courtesy. This also works for a woman treating a man with common courtesy. I know that many feminists disdain the courteous acts men have traditionally performed for women—opening doors, seating her at the table, giving her your seat at a crowded event, or offering to carry things for her. They assume such acts demean women, as if we arrogant males think females are incapable of fending for themselves.

But my own experience says otherwise. In spite of radical feminism, I find that most women appreciate these acts of courtesy and see them as tokens of respect. They make her feel womanly and cherished. They say to her, "You are highly valued. You are worthy of honor and special treatment." The foremost recipient of this kind of respect should be your wife.

Another simple way of showing respect is punctuality. Jason and Mandy show the flip side of the time and punctuality dilemma I mentioned above. It was their second anniversary, and Jason had made reservations at one of the city's most prestigious restaurants. "I'm home! Are you ready?" he called as he walked in the door.

---

*Affirming your mate's good points
and being generous with compliments
is an excellent way to show respect.*

Immediately Mandy emerged from the bedroom fully dressed, every hair in place, and all makeup applied. He was astounded. Such punctuality was not like her at all. Her failure to be ready usually made them ten to twenty minutes late anywhere they went. Mandy saw Jason's surprise and explained. "It suddenly dawned on me that my consistent lateness showed disrespect of you—of your planning, of your time, and of you as a person. I don't want to do that anymore. From now on I will work to be on time in order to give you the respect you deserve." Mandy made a bold move that produced lasting effects on the couple and on the marriage.

Affirming your mate's good points and being generous with compliments is an excellent way to show respect. When Mandy came out of that bedroom looking as dazzling as a movie star, it gave Jason a perfect opportunity to say, "Wow! You look great!" It is a simple thing, but no one ever gets tired of hearing that they look good.

Be sure, however, that the compliments go beyond appearance and focus on the heart of who she is inside. The same goes for the wife. Maybe he's all thumbs when it comes to house repairs, but that thumb is green as an Irish spring when it turns to landscaping. She should tell him how much she appreciates all he does to make their yard beautiful. And on Saturday when he comes in after spreading fertilizer, showers, and puts on his suit for a friend's wedding, she would do well to look at him with open admiration and say, "Honey, I love to see you working around the house, but when you dress up, you are the handsomest man in the world." Compliments show respect and breed respect.

RESPECTING BOUNDARIES

So far I've focused on simple but important things husbands and wives can do to show respect. Before I leave the subject, I want to address one element of respect that can loom large in any marriage: respecting boundaries.

Yes, the two of you have joined your lives together in an intimate bond. And in your lovemaking you have become—as

Moses, Christ, and Paul affirm—"one flesh" (Genesis 2:24; Matthew 19:5; 1 Corinthians 6:16). That deep intimacy and mystical oneness is vital to a marriage. But it doesn't mean that when you marry you cease to be two individual beings with certain needs unique to each of you.

Respecting boundaries means recognizing your mate's individuality. It means you willingly observe the existence of certain lines that should not be crossed. For example, mates who observe boundaries will not make decisions alone that will affect the other. She has no right to say, as I've heard wives say to neighbors, "George will be glad to come to your house on Saturday and help you build that patio." Nor does he have the right to invite his boss home for dinner without first consulting her.

Individual decisions like these cross a boundary of respect. When observing boundaries you respect each other's differing opinions and approaches. You seek input and advice before making decisions to ensure that whatever is decided does not intrude into the other's zones of safety or comfort.

Respecting boundaries means recognizing certain zones of privacy. If she has an office and he his own study, the other spouse should respect those spaces as the personally controlled domain of each. That does not mean you are not entitled to know what goes on in those places. Both should have free access to each other's computers and phones as a matter of accountability and sexual integrity.

Despite the fact that married couples make their entire bodies intimately known to each other in lovemaking, most couples feel a need for certain zones of bodily privacy. For example, using the restroom is a boundary that should be respected. And even in sex, the most intimate blending of bodies and spirits, there are boundaries to be respected, as I mentioned in chapter 2. Neither should demand of the other any act or performance that is demeaning or repelling. All acts should be mutually satisfying and bring mutual pleasure.

Both spouses are right to set boundaries against physical, verbal, or sexual abuse, and when both partners willingly observe those boundaries, each is showing love and respect.

Only when you respect each other's freedom, needs, and choices can you give yourselves lovingly to one another and bind yourselves together in the kind of intimate oneness that God intends.

AN EXPERIMENT

Things may have happened in your marriage that cause you to believe you have no reason to respect your mate. He or she has not respected you or has acted in ways that don't deserve respect. Or maybe you have simply drifted apart, each engaging in separate activities. The marriage bond has become so slack that either of you could easily slip through the loop. As a result, your spouse does not seem like the most precious person in your life. You don't feel his or her value as you did when you first married.

If any of the above is true of you, let me urge you to try a little experiment. We always treat well the things we value—that's easy to understand. But we don't generally realize that this idea can be inverted to good effect.

We will begin to value what we treat well. When you begin to treat the other person in your marriage with respect, there's a good chance it will increase your respect for him or her. By treating your mate with respect due to being created in the image of God, you will begin to see the same value God sees in that person. Another good result of showing respect is that in most cases, your mate will respond by showing more respect to you.

When you begin to treat the other person
in your marriage with respect, there's a good chance
it will increase your respect for him or her.

I realize how simplistic this may seem. Many marriages that are troubled or going flat have deeper issues that should be addressed and resolved. But if you cannot find a way to respect the person you are with, those other areas will remain as major issues for the marriage. Applying the oil of respect could do much to smooth out the everyday workings of the relation-ship, thus making the resolutions easier to work out and more likely to succeed.

And if you already have a good marriage, honing your respect can make it even better.

THINGS TO DO
TO SHOW YOUR SPOUSE RESPECT
—⟨O⟩—

- Look for things to compliment and recognize about your spouse.

- Model respectful behavior with everyone in your family, but especially your spouse.

- Help your spouse know things to do to show you respect.

- Whenever possible show your respect for the things that are respectful about your spouse. Point out and focus on any positive change your spouse makes.

- Continue to explore new ways of raising respect such as involvement in new and interesting projects and hobbies.

- Self-respect results in respect for others.

Notes

Chapter 1

1. Alyson Weasley, "The Role of Friendship in Marriage," Focus on the Family, http://www.focusonthefamily.com/marriage/sex_and_intimacy/the_role_of_friendship_in_marriage.aspx.
2. Bill and Pam Farrel, *Red-Hot Monogamy* (Eugene, OR: Harvest House, 2006).
3. James R. White with Peter Kent, *The Best Sex of Your Life* (Fort Lee, NJ: Barricade Books, 1997) 91.
4. Bill and Pam Farrel, "Recreational Intimacy," Focus on the Family, http://www.focusonthefamily.com/marriage/daily_living/making-time-for-romance-and-intimacy/recreational-intimacy.aspx.

Chapter 2

1. Christopher West, *At the Heart of the Gospel* (New York: Image Books, 2012), 190.
2. Peter Paul Rubens, *Adam and Eve*, Peter Paul Rubens: The Complete Works, http://www.peterpaulrubens.org/Adam-and-Eve.html.
3. Lucas Cranach the Elder, *Eve*, Olga's Gallery, http://www.abcgallery.com/C/cranach/cranach66.html.

Chapter 4

1. Adapted from Jim Bradford, "Marriage: Accepting, not Judging," Assemblies of God USA, February 1, 2012. http://agtv.ag.org/marriage_accepting_not_judging.

Chapter 5

1. Gary Smalley, *Making Love Last Forever* (Nashville: Thomas Nelson, 1997).
2. Dave Ramsey, "Money Talk: The 'You' in 'Unity' Is Silent," Focus on the Family, http://www.focusonthefamily.com/marriage/money_and_finances/pursuing_financial_unity/money_talk_the_you_in_unity_is_silent.aspx.
3. Crown Financial Ministries, "Financial Authority," Focus on the Family website, adapted from Larry Burkett, "Financial Authority in the Home," in *Biblical Principles Under Scrutiny* (Chicago: Moody, 1990), 177–179, http://www.focusonthefamily.com/marriage/money_and_finances/money_management_in_marriage/financial_authority.aspx.
4. Ben Woolsey and Matt Schulz, "Credit card statistics, industry facts, debt statistics," CreditCards.com; http://www.creditcards.com/creditcard-news/credit-card-industry-facts-personal-debt-statistics-1276.php.

5. Carolyn MacInnes, "Big Dreams on a Small Budget," Focus on the Family, http://www.focusonthefamily.com/marriage/money_and_finances/money_management_in_marriage/big_dreams_on_a_small_budget.aspx.

Chapter 6

1. Emil Protalinski, "Facebook Blamed for 1 in 5 Divorces in the US," ZDNet, March 1, 2011, http://www.zdnet.com/blog/facebookfacebook-blamed-for-1-in-5-divorces-in-the-us/359.
2. Willard F. Harley, "The Four Rules for a Successful Marriage," Marriage Builders, accessed June 11, 2012, http://www.marriagebuilders.com/graphic/mbi3901_rules.html.
3. Adapted from Harley, "The Four Rules for a Successful Marriage."
4. "Major New Study: Does Divorce Make People Unhappy? Findings from a Study of Unhappy Marriages," undated press release, AmericanValues.org, http://www.americanvalues.org/html/r-unhappy_ii.html.
5. DivorceStatistics.org, accessed December 28, 2011.
6. Ed Cray, *General of the Army: George C. Marshall, Soldier and Statesman* (New York: W. W. Norton, 1990), 89.

Chapter 7

1. C. S. Lewis, "The Weight of Glory" in *The Weight of Glory and Other Addresses* (New York: Macmillan, 1949), 19.

About the Author

STEPHEN ARTERBURN is a best-selling and award-winning author with over eight million books in print. His popular titles include *Every Man's Battle* and *Healing Is a Choice*. He has also been the editor of ten Bible projects, including *The Life Recovery Bible*. Arterburn founded New Life Treatment Centers in 1988 and is currently host of the radio and television show *New Life Live*. In 1996 he started the successful traveling conference Women of Faith, which has been attended by more than four million people. He and his wife live with their five kids in Fishers, Indiana.

NEW LIFE MARRIAGE WEEKEND WORKSHOP

🌿 *Rejuvenate*　　　✚ *Rescue*　　　🫀 *Restore*

There is hope for your marriage!

- Do you want the tools to make a great marriage?

- Do you need to repair love that's been broken?

- Do you want a deeper spiritual and emotional intimacy?

Designed to take the focus from what was and what might have been and onto the path of what is and what is to be. All workshop attendees will attend process groups where they will work on their issues of concern with a Christian counselor and fellow attendees.

for information or to register call

800-NEW-LIFE (639-5433) **newlife.com**

WORTHY®
Inspired

If you enjoyed this book, will you consider sharing
the message with others?

- Mention the book in a Facebook post, Twitter update, Pinterest pin, blog post, or upload a picture through Instagram.
- Recommend this book to those in your small group, book club, workplace, and classes.
- Head over to facebook.com/NewLifeLive, "LIKE" the page, and post a comment as to what you enjoyed the most.
- Pick up a copy for someone you know who would be challenged and encouraged by this message.
- Write a review on amazon.com, bn.com, goodreads.com, or cbd.com.

You can subscribe to Worthy Publishing's
newsletter at worthypublishing.com.

Worthy Publishing Facebook Page   Worthy Publishing Website